Angels and Demons:
From Creation To Armageddon

By Joseph Lumpkin

Angels and Demons: From Creation to Armageddon

Copyright © 2009 by Joseph Lumpkin

All rights reserved.

Fifth Estate, Post Office Box 116,

Blountsville, AL 35031

First Edition

Cover Designed by An Quigley

Printed on acid-free paper

Library of Congress Control No: 2009927932

ISBN: 9781933580685

Fifth Estate, 2009

Table of Contents

Introduction   7

In The Beginning   9

A Little Angelic History   10

Setting the Stage   22

The Alpha   67

Panoramic View   89

Story of Evil   90

The Omega   158

About the Ancient Texts   159

Appendix "A"   193

Appendix "B"   199

Appendix "C"   211

Appendix "D"   235

Introduction

In 2006 Fifth Estate Publishers released the book, "Fallen Angels, The Watchers, and the Origins of Evil." The book met with wide success, with only one criticism. It was too short. People desired more information. It is with this in mind that we present "Angels and Demons: From Creation to Armageddon."

Since the writing of the first book, several new texts have been translated and explored, including the Books of Adam and Eve, The Book of the Giants, and the Second Book of Enoch, also called the Book of the Secrets of Enoch. In addition, many other sources of information have been accessed in order to better explain the history and theories behind the existence of Angels and Demons.

As with any story, there are three basic ways of viewing the content. Allowing for the human propensity to elaborate, one must decide if the tale being told is true, fictitious, or accurate only in as far as the writer is aware or can explain.

Whether the reader decides the stories and facts presented in this book actually pertain to angels in the spiritual sense, or if the ancient authors were attempting to explain the existence of visitors from other times or places, whose science appeared to be magic, the fragments of texts herein will shed light on possible interpretations.

By placing the texts in chronological order, and removing the parts of the texts not pertaining to spirits and gods, we can form a timeline of the activities of angels, their fall, and the subsequent activities of those fallen angels we call demons.

Disclaimer

Even though my degree is in Ministry, most of my working life has been spent in the computer field. For the last seven years I have been employed as an analyst in the "Hypersonic Missile Technology" project, which is part of the Department of Defense. What this time taught me was that very intelligent people always assume they never have all of the data and any assumptions could be wrong. We are allowed our opinions but should keep an eternally open mind. Add to all of this the fact that technology continues to convert magic of today into the reality of tomorrow and we have a formula of uncertainty regarding descriptions of "Angels, Demons, and gods" in ancient texts.

Being a person raised and educated in "traditional Christianity" always believed that those entities mentioned in the Bible under the names of Angels, Seraphim, and Cherubim are exactly as the scriptures describe them – spiritual beings made by God for His service. Demons are those same beings acting contrary to their natural purpose. However, there are many unanswered questions and coincidental occurrences. Thus, even though I have my own personal opinion, I entertain the possibility that I could be wrong.

Presented to the reader is the data from history and ancient texts, which forced me to question my own traditional beliefs. I draw no conclusions but only ask those questions I have asked myself. Whether one starts with a totally open mind, or with an assumption that the beings in the pages of history are from God, a different space, time, or dimension, it is my belief that the reader is wise enough to make up his or her own mind.

To enable the reader to further investigate the fascinating subject of angels and demons, the books quoted or used in the research of this work are cited along with a brief description of the individual texts in the chapter entitled, "About the Ancient Texts."

Admittedly, the first section of this book is filled with various unrelated texts that sets a stage to open the reader to the possibilities of what or who Angels could be, but this makes the first chapters read like a flat tire rolls. The story told in the following chapter will hopefully make it all worth the read. It is an amazing story.

In The Beginning

As it is today, those who do good deeds or perform their duty, always seem to get less attention than those who are evil or rebellious. So it is with the heavenly hosts. Angels may have headlines in the Bible, but not in secular books, and certainly not on the movie screen. In general, there is less information available about angels than their fallen and corrupt counterparts. Sex and violence sells and it sold in 200 B.C.E just as well. As we will see later, this was also the case in the ancient world and it becomes obvious as we place the texts in chronological order to develop a storyline of angels and demons.

It is not clear when angels were created. The creation of birds, fish, animals, and plants are mentioned in the book of Genesis. The creation of man was covered in two complete storylines in Genesis, but the creation of angels deserved no mention. We can assume the creation of all spiritual creatures took place at the same time heaven was created, on the first day.

We know that heavenly creatures are grouped into three divisions in the Bible of angels, seraphim, and cherubim. Although later, at the end of the tenth century, Rabbi Moshe ben Maimon," (1135-1204), court physician to Sultan Saladin of Egypt and author of a commentary on the Mishnah, the Book of Mitzvot, Mishneh Torah, the Guide to the Perplexed, and many other works, divided all angels into ten ranks. Namely: Chayot Hakodesh, Ophanim, Erelim, Chashmalim, Seraphim, Malachim, Elokim, Bene Elokim, Cheruvim, and Ishim.

These ranks refer to the degree of the angel's comprehension of or proximity to God. His thought was that some have a greater understanding of God and His ways than others. The Rabbi likely took his ideas from the nine degrees of angels taught by the theologians of the Middle East in the 5th century, and later by the Catholic Church in the 6th century.

A Little Angelic History

According to Jewish tradition, an angel is a spiritual being and does not have any physical characteristics. The angelic descriptions provided by the prophets – such as wings, arms etc. – are anthropomorphic connections to their spiritual abilities and tasks.

The first angels mentioned by name in the Bible are Gabriel and Michael, in the Book of Daniel. The Jerusalem Talmud comments that reference to angels by name only became common in the period following the return of the Jewish people to Israel in 348 BCE. In the Talmud and Kabbala many more angels are identified by name. Some other commonly known names of angels include Uriel, Reziel, Metatron, and Laila. In the Apocrypha Raphael is mentioned, and in the Lost Book of Enoch the leaders of the fallen angels, also referred to as the Watchers are listed by name.

The Hebrew word for angel is *"malach,"* (malak) which means messenger, for the angels are God's messengers. Every angel is created to perform certain tasks; such as announcements, judgments, healing, and other tasks. According to the Zohar one of the angels' tasks is to transport our words of prayer and Bible study before God's throne.

There are Christian sects that place Jesus into the same group, calling him an angel. Since the English word "angel" comes from the Greek "angelos," which means 'messenger,' and in the Old Testament, with two exceptions, the Hebrew word malak, also meaning 'messenger,' and the Old testament spoke about the coming of "the messenger of the covenant", Jesus Christ (Malachi 3:1), it is said by some that Jesus was an angel. To take this to its ultimate conclusion, the Church of Jesus Christ of Latter Day Saints (The

Mormons), view Jesus and Lucifer as brothers.

Joseph Fielding Smith Jr.,the LDS prophet, wrote in his work, Doctrines of Salvation, Vol.2, Pg.218 -Pg.219

"We learn from the scriptures that Lucifer -- once a son of the morning, who exercised authority in the presence of God before the foundations of this earth were laid -- rebelled against the plan of salvation and against Jesus Christ who was chosen to be the Savior of the world and who is spoken of as the 'Lamb slain from the foundation of the world.'"

In the Discourses of Brigham Young, on Pg.53-54 he lets it be known that Lucifer is the second son, the one known as "Son of the Morning."

"Who will redeem the earth, who will go forth and make the sacrifice for the earth and all things it contains?" The Eldest Son said: "Here am I"; and then he added, "Send me." But the second one, which was "Lucifer, Son of the Morning," said, "Lord, here am I, send me, I will redeem every son and daughter of Adam and Eve that lives on the earth, or that ever goes on the earth."

Bruce R. McConkie, in his work The Mortal Messiah, Vol.1, Pg.407-408 under the heading " Lucifer and the Law of Temptation" has the following to say;

"Hence, there is -- and must be -- a devil, and he is the father of lies and of wickedness. He and the fallen angels who followed him are spirit children of the Father. As Christ is the Firstborn of the Father in the spirit, so Lucifer is a son of the morning, one of those born in the morning of preexistence. He is a spirit man, a personage, an entity, comparable in form and appearance to any of the spirit children of the Eternal Father. He was the source of opposition among the spirit hosts before the world was made; he rebelled in preexistence against the Father and the Son, and he sought even then to destroy the agency of man. He and his followers were cast down to earth, and they are forever denied mortal bodies. And he, here on earth, along with all who follow him -- both his spirit followers and the mortals who hearken to his enticements -- is continuing the war that commenced in heaven."

In the work of Otten & Caldwell, Sacred Truths of the Doctrine & Covenants, Vol.2, Pg.28 it is found that Lucifer rebelled against his "Heavenly Father."

"We also learn that Lucifer ... was in authority..." in the premortal life. (See D&C 76:25) Authority in the presence of God is known to us as priesthood. In other words, Lucifer held the priesthood. We know that Lucifer rebelled against his Heavenly Father. One of the great insights given in this vision was the way this rebellion was manifested."

Through reading John A. Widtsoe's work Evidences and Reconciliations, Pg.209, it is learned that Lucifer strove to gain the birthright of his Elder Brother, Jesus the Christ and became Satan, the enemy of God.

"The story of Lucifer is the most terrible example of such apostasy. Lucifer, son of the morning, through diligent search for truth and the use of it, had become one of the foremost in the assembly of those invited to undertake the experiences of earth. But, in that Great Council, his personal ambition and love of power overcame him. He pitted his own plan and will against the purposes of God. He strove to gain the birthright of his Elder Brother, Jesus the Christ. When his proposition was rejected, he forsook all that he had gained, would not repent of his sin, defied truth, and of necessity lost his place among the followers of God. He was no longer Lucifer, bearer of truth, who walked in light, but Satan, teacher of untruth, who slunk in darkness. He became the enemy of God and of all who try to walk according to the Lord's commandments. One-third of the spirits present in that vast assembly supported Satan and became enemies of the truth that they had formerly cherished. With him these rebellious spirits lost their fellowship with the valiant sons of God. What is more, they lost the privilege of obtaining bodies of flesh and blood, without which they cannot gain full power over the forces of the universe. In the face of that defeat, and that curse, they have sought from Adam to the present time to corrupt mankind and defeat the Lord's purposes."

Jewish tradition holds that there are also angels who argue our case to God, and those who accuse us. It is written, "He who fulfills one good deed of human kindness, acquires for himself one angel-advocate; he who commits one transgression, acquires against himself one angel-accuser."

According to some schools of thought, the term angel in Jewish literature can also refer to the angels who control nature, or to natural powers given the symbol of an angelic or human form, which are endowed with Godly powers. This explains how there may be many types of angels.

We are told that angels continually sing praises around the throne of God. The type of praise they sing reflects the particular angel's spiritual status. The angels' singing is alluded to in the story of Jacob's fight with the angel, at the end of which the angel pleaded with Jacob to free him "for the dawn has risen." According to the Midrash, the angels have "shifts," singing at designated times of day or night. The angel's rush was because his shift to sing before God had arrived.

One of the great controversies regarding angels is the problem of free will. Many ancient Jewish teachers espoused a view that angels were somewhat "one dimensional" creatures, made for a particular propose and possessing no free will. Although prima facie this seems suitable, it leaves us with no explanation as to how Lucifer could choose his own path of pride and have the will to rebel and attempt to set up a kingdom of his own with followers he had gathered to himself. Further, if we give Satan an elevated status, calling him the crown of creation, to give the gift of free will to him alone does not account for the ability of one-third of the angels to follow him in his war against the God who made them all. In the end, we may see the angels are much like ourselves, created with purpose in mind, but with free will to fulfill or deny their destiny.

Using the Bible containing the Apocrypha, we can parse the verses mentioning or describing angels so as to form an overview of what the Bible has to say about angels. The first thing to notice is that there are three major divisions of spiritual creatures mentioned in the Bible: Cherubim, Seraphim, and Angels. Angels seem the have a military rank and file assignment with a handful of commanders called, Archangels. Angels are simply servants and messengers.

Cherubim: (cherubim is the Hebrew masculine plural)
There are two schools of thought as to what the word, "Cherubim" actually means. Cherubim could mean, "The Seat of the Glory of God", and is interpreted: Fullness of Knowledge. This could be due to the fact that they serve near the throne of God and are positioned on the mercy seat of the ark.

The word cherub could also be a word borrowed from the Assyrian kirubu, or karâbu, meaning, "to be near." The word and therefore the being has come to designate the heavenly creatures serving close to the throne of God, who closely surrounded God and pay Him service.

Exodus 25:18-21 - Cherubim were placed on the kapporeth, or lid of the Ark, called "the Mercy-Seat." The figures were of two cherubim made of gold.

1 Kings 6:23 and 2 Chronicles 3:11 - Solomon placed in the Holy of Holies two huge Cherubim of olive-wood overlaid with gold. "They stood on their feet and their faces were towards the house", which probably means they faced the Holy Place or the Entrance.

Exod., 26:31 - Cherubim were embroidered on the Veil of the Tabernacle, separating the Holy Place from the Holy of Holies. "With blue and purple and scarlet and fine twined linen" they were made. They were two large-sized figures representing guardian spirits.

From Ezekiel 10:4 it can be concluded that a cherub's appearance could not have been a human one, since the figure is described as having a face of a man, and face of a cherubim, and the face of an animal. The verse reads, "the first face was the face of a cherub and the second that of a man, the third the face of a lion and the fourth the face of an eagle."

The representation of the cherubim may have been barrowed from Egyptian art and deities of the time. Figures with a human face and two outstretched wings attached to the arms are very common. Hawk-headed figures are common in Assyrian art. These are winged human figures standing beside a palm tree. Josephus tells us that the Jews had forgotten what the figure was supposed to really look like and the Bible gives no word of explanation. However, it may not have described the figure because it was at one time ubiquitous and among the most common figures of contemporary art.

Whatever the history and time line of the belief in Cherubim, we know they were well set in the Jewish psyche no later than 200 B.C.E., owing to the records of "The Lost Book of Enoch" (First Enoch) and the "Apocryphal Book of Esdras."

Seraphim: (Hebrew masculine plural form)

The name is derived from the Hebrew verb saraph, "to consume with fire."

The title, "Seraphim," designates a special class of heavenly attendants, each having six wings: two to bear them up, two cover their faces, and two covering their feet. They were naked, as was the custom to serve in the presence of God, symbolizing vulnerability. These were His highest servants. They were there to minister to Him and proclaim His glory as they shouted to one another and to all that could hear, "Holy! Holy! Holy! Lord of Hosts, the Earth is full of His glory…" In Isaiah 6:6 a seraphim flew towards the prophet bearing a live coal, which he had taken from the altar. He touched and purified the prophet's lips with the coal, symbolizing that henceforth his word would be holy and of inspiration.

The Seraphim are around the throne in a double choir and the volume of their singing shakes the foundations of the throne. They are distinct from the cherubim. The seraphim stand before God as ministering servants around the throne. Although it is difficult to obtain from the single passage any clear, concise description of them.

As mentioned, many theologians think the name, Seraphim, is derived from the Hebrew verb *sarap*, meaning, "to consume with fire." This etymology is probable because of Isaiah 6:6, where one of the seraphim is represented as carrying a burning coal of holy fire from the altar to purify the Prophet's lips. However, many scholars prefer to derive it from the Hebrew noun *saraph*, "a fiery and flying serpent", spoken of in Numbers 21:6

and Isaiah 14:29, which speaks of the brazen image, which stood in the Temple in the time of Isaiah's time, as described in 2 Kings 18:4.

The seraphim and cherubim are mentioned at least twice in the Book of Enoch. In early Christian Theology, the cherubim and seraphim occupy the highest rank in the heavenly hierarchy.

Later, the cherubim and seraphim were sometimes thought to be other names for thrones and virtues. These were from a list of nine types of angels, developed in the early sixth century A.D. The listing of the Nine Angelic Choirs for angels was developed by a theologian named Pseudo-Dionysius the Areopagite, in the book "Celestial Hierarchy," and was endorsed and accepted by Thomas Aquinas in his book, Summa Theologica, in the thirteenth century. They are mentioned in the Bible, but it is not obvious that all of the stations mentioned refer to beings and not states of being.

The names of the choirs are:

Seraphim, Cherubim, Thrones, Dominions, Virtues, Powers, Principalities, Archangels, and Angels.

Some may take exception to the inclusion of "Virtues, Dominions, or "Thrones" being in the list of types of angels. They appear to be more locations or states of being rather than beings themselves. The church fathers disagreed.

Many modern scholars attempt to exaggerate the obsession of the early church about subjects they could never prove by referencing the age-old question of "How many angels can dance on the head of a pin?" To be fair, this particular question has never been found. The modern version in English dates back at least to Richard Baxter in his 1667 tract "The Reasons of the Christian Religion." Baxter questions the ability and powers of angels to exist in a material world, concluding "And Schibler with others, maketh the difference of extension to be this, that Angels can contract their whole substance into one part of space, and therefore take up virtually no space. Whereupon it is that the Schoolmen have questioned how many Angels may fit upon the point of a Needle?" This proves only that to the extent of our science, wisdom, and capacity of critical thinking, man has sought to discover and know more about angels for centuries.

Since Pseudo-Dionysius had espoused his angelic stations around A.D. 500, the nine divisions of the angelic order had been accepted and made universal. The angelic order was built on the work St. Cyril of Jerusalem in 370 A.D. and St. Chrysostom in about 400 A.D. These men were part of the Eastern Church. Pseudo-Dionysius made it fashionable; Pope Gregory made the angelic order familiar to the Western Churches.

Angels have an important place in the Christian religion and the bible is replete with references to those who provide enlightenment and spiritual guidance. Based on passages in the New Testament and the fifth century writings of Dionysius the Areopagite, theologians in the Middle Ages developed a classification containing different levels of angels, dividing them into nine categories known as 'angelic choirs'. The hierarchy is as follows:

First level

This is the highest level of angels and therefore the closest to God. These enlightened celestial beings have the deepest understanding of divinity and manifest to humans as a beam of pure, shining light, too holy to be looked upon.

Seraphim – protectors of God's divinity, spreading His word through praise and song and surrounding His throne, Cherubim – guardians of light and stars and providers of divine love and wisdom, Ophanim – portals of God's intellect and full of divine knowledge, these angels are also known as 'thrones.'

Second level

Angels in the second level of the hierarchy function as heavenly governors, presiding over existence on earth without manifesting their existence to humans.

Dominions – also known as hashmallim. These angels take orders from the first level in order to lead the lower ranks of angels and watch over earthly existence. Virtues – the source of spiritual power and often thought of as 'miracle angels', these heavenly beings guide human spiritual growth. Powers – regulate the course of history on the earth to ensure that God's will is carried out.

Third level

These angels are spiritual messengers, acting as a link between God and humankind, carrying God's will and word to the world.

Principalities – guide countries and nation groups to keep the earth in balance.

Archangels – provide guidance in matters of great human importance. Angels – these are the angels with whom we are most familiar, as they are concerned with all matters in our personal lives. They guide everyone on earth, whether we know it or not.

The Scriptures below contain the nine levels or choirs of heavenly beings, which are:

Seraphim, Cherubim, Thrones, Dominions, Virtues, Powers, Principalities, Archangels, and Angels. It should be noted here that if an angel gives his name and is singled out for a great mission he is considered an archangel. Other angels serve below this post as part of the army or host of angels.

Isaiah 6:1 (6:1) In the year king Uzziah died, I saw the Lord seated on a high and lofty throne, with the train of his garment filling the temple. (6:2) **Seraphim** were stationed above; each one of them had six wings: with two they veiled their faces, with two they veiled their feet, and with two they hovered aloft. (6:3) "Holy, holy, holy is the Lord of hosts " they cried one to the other. "All the earth is filled with his glory!"

Genesis (3:23) The Lord God therefore banished him (Adam) from the garden of Eden, to till the ground from which he had been taken. (3:24) When he expelled the man, he settled him east of the garden of Eden; and he stationed the **Cherubim** and the fiery revolving sword, to guard the way to the tree of life.

Colossians 1:16. In him everything in heaven and on earth was created, things visible and invisible, whether **thrones or dominions, principalities or powers**, all were created through him, and for him. (1:20) It is like the strength he showed in raising Christ from the dead and seating him at his right hand in heaven, (1:21) high above every **principality, power, virtue, and dominion**, and every name that can be given in this age or in the age to come.

Revelation 12:7. Then war broke out in heaven; **Michael and his angels** battled against the dragon. Although the dragon and his angels fought back 12:8) they were overpowered and lost their place in heaven 12:9) The huge dragon, the ancient serpent known as the devil or Satan, the seducer of the whole world, was driven out; he was hurled down to earth and his minions with him.

Tobit (12:12) I can now tell you that when you, Tobit, and Sarah prayed, it was I who presented and read the record of your prayers before the Glory of the Lord; and I did the same thing when you used to bury the dead. (12:14) At the same time, however, **God commissioned me to heal you and your daughter-in-law Sarah.** 12:15) I am Raphael, **one of the seven angels who enter and serve before the glory of the Lord.**

Luke (1:26) "And in the sixth month the **angel Gabriel** was sent from God unto a city of Galilee, named Nazareth, (1:27) To a virgin espoused to a man whose name was Joseph, of the house of David; and the virgin's name was Mary.

Matthew 18:10 "See that you despise not one of these little ones; for I say to you that **their angels in Heaven** always see the face of My Father Who is in Heaven"
This verse is used to prove the existence of guardian angels.

For a complete list of Biblical references to angels, including those in the Apocrypha, please see Appendix "C."

Setting the Stage

Three times creation fell. Three times Gods declared a separation; once in heaven, once on earth, and once between the two. Three times, God's creation violated his will, so the earth and all therein suffered, or so we are told.

There was a great war in heaven and Lucifer, prince of the angels, declared his intention to seize the throne of the Most High God. Fueled by arrogance and pride, he whipped up support, promising one-third of the angels a place in his new kingdom if they followed him. It was a choice to serve God or rule a piece of what would be left after heaven was destroyed. They thought it better to rule in chaos than serve in paradise. The war was on.

But, his plan did not work. Even though Lucifer was the pinnacle of God's angelic creation and the greatest of all angels, he could not defeat the warrior Michael and the army that remained, for God empowered the host advancing his will.

With the rage of the vanquished-prideful, Lucifer, now known as Satan, continued his attack, not against the heavenly host that had defeated him, but against the helpless creation of the God he so hated. This was to be the cause of the fall of man.

Part of the heavenly host, still obedient to God, were fulfilling their appointed duties. These were called "The Watchers." They were assigned to record the deeds of man and watch over the creation, accounting for its activities. It was after the fall of the angels and after the fall of man, when mankind began to populate the earth, that the Watchers noticed the emerging beauty of the human women. These spiritual beings saw the women of the earth and wanted them. They sought to taste the love and lust that drove men. So they did, and 200 Watchers fell from the spiritual world to the baser physical realm. The consequences would literally haunt mankind forever.

Let us examine this story in it's individual sections.

(Revelation 12:7-17)

"And war broke out in heaven: Michael and his angels fought against the dragon; and the dragon and his angels fought, but they did not prevail, nor was a place found for them in heaven any longer. So the great dragon who was cast out, that serpent of old, called the Devil and Satan, who deceives the whole world; he was cast to the earth, and his angels were cast out with him.

Then I heard a loud voice saying in heaven, "Now salvation, and strength, and the kingdom of our God, and the power of His Christ have come, for the accuser of our brethren, who accused them before our God day and night, has been cast down ... Therefore rejoice, O heavens, and you who dwell in them!

Woe to the inhabitants of the earth and the sea! For the devil has come down to you, having great wrath, because he knows that he has a short time.

Now when the dragon saw that he had been cast to the earth, he persecuted the woman who gave birth to the male child. But the woman was given two wings of a great eagle, that she might fly into the wilderness to her place, where she is nourished for a time and times and half a time, from the presence of the serpent.

So the serpent spewed water out of his mouth like a flood after the woman, that he might cause her to be carried away by the flood. But the earth helped the woman, and the earth opened its mouth and swallowed up the flood, which the dragon had spewed out of his mouth.

And the dragon was enraged with the woman, and he went to make war with the rest of her offspring, who keep the commandments of God and have the testimony of Jesus Christ."

(The "woman" mentioned in the above verse is Israel. The "male child" that the woman had given birth to is Jesus. The wings given to the woman represent the grace of God affording a victorious outcome.)

Genesis 3

"1 Now the serpent was more crafty than any of the wild animals the LORD God had made. He said to the woman, "Did God really say, 'You must not eat from any tree in the garden'?"

2 The woman said to the serpent, "We may eat fruit from the trees in the garden, 3 but God did say, 'You must not eat fruit from the tree that is in the middle of the garden, and you must not touch it, or you will die.' "

4 "You will not surely die," the serpent said to the woman. 5 "For God knows that when you eat of it your eyes will be opened, and you will be like God, knowing good and evil."

6 When the woman saw that the fruit of the tree was good for food and pleasing to the eye, and also desirable for gaining wisdom, she took some and ate it. She also gave some to her husband, who was with her, and he ate it. 7 Then the eyes of both of them were opened, and they realized they were naked; so they sewed fig leaves together and made coverings for themselves.

8 Then the man and his wife heard the sound of the LORD God as he was walking in the garden in the cool of the day, and they hid from the LORD God among the trees of the garden. 9 But the LORD God called to the man, "Where are you?"

10 He answered, "I heard you in the garden, and I was afraid because I was naked; so I hid."

11 And he said, "Who told you that you were naked? Have you eaten from

the tree that I commanded you not to eat from?"

12 The man said, "The woman you put here with me—she gave me some fruit from the tree, and I ate it."

13 Then the LORD God said to the woman, "What is this you have done?" The woman said, "The serpent deceived me, and I ate."

14 So the LORD God said to the serpent, "Because you have done this, "Cursed are you above all the livestock and all the wild animals! You will crawl on your belly and you will eat dust all the days of your life.

15 And I will put enmity between you and the woman, and between your offspring and hers; he will crush your head, and you will strike his heel."

16 To the woman he said, "I will greatly increase your pains in childbearing; with pain you will give birth to children. Your desire will be for your husband, and he will rule over you."

17 To Adam he said, "Because you listened to your wife and ate from the tree about which I commanded you, 'You must not eat of it,' "Cursed is the ground because of you; through painful toil you will eat of it all the days of your life.

18 It will produce thorns and thistles for you, and you will eat the plants of the field.

19 By the sweat of your brow you will eat your food until you return to the ground, since from it you were taken; for dust you are and to dust you will return."

20 Adam named his wife Eve, because she would become the mother of all the living.

21 The LORD God made garments of skin for Adam and his wife and clothed them. 22 And the LORD God said, "The man has now become like one of us, knowing good and evil. He must not be allowed to reach out his hand and take also from the tree of life and eat, and live forever." 23 So the LORD God banished him from the Garden of Eden to work the ground from which he had been taken. 24 After he drove the man out, he placed on

the east side of the Garden of Eden cherubim and a flaming sword flashing back and forth to guard the way to the tree of life."

Why would God forbid knowledge? Why would the pursuit of knowledge mean the punishment of exile and even death? What did the creator want to keep hidden from mankind? Some say it was the creator's real identity, because the god who created Adam was not the true God at all, but an angel gone mad, jealous, and desiring to be worshiped as God.

This is articulated in other versions of creation. These long hidden and secret books tell of a god that is quite mad. The stories tell of a god who fought to keep mankind ignorant and enslaved. In this story one god fought another for the soul of man and man's right to be free. Both of these deities were what we would call "angels" because, according to the people who recorded the events, both gods were themselves created by a sovereign God.

Questions must arise. Were these "gods" actually angels or an advanced race? Could there not have been a difference of opinion within the leadership as to whether their identities should be revealed or whether some basic modicum of knowledge could be shared with man in order to help humanity advance and assure its survival? It appears that the angel who directed Adam's creation wished to keep him ignorant, but Jesus came to give us knowledge. He knew that if he opened Adam's eyes to the sacred knowledge of the true God he would become stronger than his creator angel.

But what they call "the tree of knowledge of good and evil" is the Thought of the light. They (the angels) stationed themselves in front of it so that Adam might not understand his fullness and recognize his nakedness and be ashamed. But it was I (Jesus) who made them decide what they ate.

I said to the savior, Lord, wasn't it the serpent that instructed Adam to eat? The savior smiled and said, The serpent instructed them to eat because of its evil desire to produced sexual lust and destruction so that Adam would be useful to him. Adam knew that he was disobedient to Yaldaboth (the god that created man) because the light of the Thought lived in him and made him stronger and more accurate in his thinking than the head Archon (power). Yaldaboth wanted to harvest the power that he himself had given Adam. And he caused Adam to forget.

And I said to the savior, "What is this forgetfulness?" He said, "It is not how Moses wrote and it is not how you have heard. He wrote in his first book, 'He put him to sleep' (Genesis 2:21), but that was how Adam perceived it. For also he said through the prophet, 'I will make their minds heavy, that they may not perceive nor understand.' (Isaiah 6:10)."
The Apocryphon of John
From the book, "The Gnostic Scriptures," published by Fifth Estate Publishers.

In this astonishing story there are multiple "deities." Yaldaboth is the god who created the earth and man. He is viewed as being insane and cruel, wishing to keep Adam ignorant so he would serve and worship Yaldaboth forever. Jesus wished to free man, to reveal knowledge to him, and allow him to grow. This is Gnostic theology. (See the Gnostic Scriptures, published by Fifth Estate.)

Gnosticism is a Christian sect that acknowledges a hierarchy of deities with a supreme creative force at its zenith. But it was not the supreme "god" who created mankind. No indeed, because this world and the functioning of it was viewed as being illogical, defective, and insane.

Bad things happened to good people, and evil overcomes good too often. In the Gnostic view of the world, the god who created this world was inferior. He desired to keep mankind in darkness and ignorance so man would be forever trapped in the illusion that the god they spoke to was the only god and the true god. He wished to forbid the growth of wisdom and knowledge of man. He wished to keep them as pets, forever. Other gods thought differently. Jesus was the highest creation, formed from the pinnacle of thought from the spirit of a supreme God. Jesus wished man to be free through the knowledge of the existence of the one true God.

If the idea of multiple deities within a monotheistic religion such as Christianity is unsettling to you, look closer at the Bible.

God standeth in the Congregation of God (El)
In the midst of gods (elohim) He judgeth
All the foundations of the earth are moved.
I said: Ye are gods,
And all of you sons of the Most High (Elyon)
Nevertheles ye shall die like men,
And fall like one of the princes (sarim)
Psalm 82:1, 5-7

As this verse implies, there seem to be multiple gods produced by a single superior creative entity, and like any family – some offspring are simply evil.

Is mankind caught in a war between gods, as Gnostic scriptures suggest? Are these "gods" the ones who taught us how to build, work metals, use herbs, read the seasons, make war, as well as how to write? Did they bring us the knowledge needed to build the towers and pyramids of the ancient world? Where did they come from? Who are they? What do they want? Are they good or evil? And, if some are truly evil, what is the definition of evil?

A sect called the Cathars attempted to answer these questions. They wrote and collected books, building a library. Thirteen papyri from this library were discovered near the town of Nag Hammadi in 1945 by a peasant boy. The writings in these codices comprised 52 documents, most of which are Gnostic in nature.

The codices were probably hidden by monks from the nearby monastery of St. Pachomius when the official Christian Church banned all Gnostic literature around the year 390 A.D

It is believed the original texts were written in Greek during the first or second centuries A.D. The copies contained in the discovered clay jar were written in Coptic in the third or fourth centuries A.D.

From the time Gnosticism was labeled a heresy, the church began a policy of conversion or extermination. Beginning around 390 A.D. and continuing until the Cathar extermination, the church opposed Gnosticism and all movements, forms, and sects that proceeded from it.

In 1209 Pope Innocent III proclaimed a crusade against the last vestiges of "Gnostic-like" sects, the Cathars. For years the church discussed the Cathars, attempting to decide if they could be considered Christian or not. Eventually they would be labeled heretical and ordered to come into line with the orthodox beliefs of the Catholic Church.

The Cathars held to their beliefs. Their doctrine included the belief that the world was split along lines of matter and spirit, good and evil. As with many Gnostic sects, they believed in abstaining from the world by purifying themselves, living a life of chastity and poverty. They believed in the equality of the sexes. They believed in the pursuit of truth and knowledge.

The Pope saw the Cathars as a danger to the church since the members were admired for their modest lifestyle and the Cathar membership was growing quickly.

Even though the Cathars were an ascetic sect, leading lives of peace and abstinence, they were hunted down and killed. Twenty years of carnage and warfare followed in which cities and provinces throughout the south of France were systematically eradicated in an attempt to kill every Cathar. One of the worst episodes of the war ensued when the entire population of Toulouse, both Cathar and Catholic, were massacred. In 1243 the Cathar fortress of Montsegur in the Pyrenees was captured and destroyed. Those who refused to renounce their beliefs were tortured or put to death by fire. In spite of continued persecution, the Cathar movement continued through the 14th century, finally disappearing in the 15th century. Still, the church could not find or destroy all Gnostic literature.

The content of their Gnostic teaching surprised most. Gnosticism claims special knowledge of creation and the evolution of man.

From the book, The Apocryphon of John, we read:

This is the five-fold creation of the kingdom of the Father, which is the first man and the image of the invisible Spirit, which came from Barbelo, who was the divine Thought; Forethought, Foreknowledge, Indestructibility, Eternal life, and Truth.

This is the androgynous five-fold being of the kingdom, which is the ten types of kingdoms, which is the Father.

(Five, being both male and female, or neither male nor female, become ten.)

And he looked at Barbelo with his pure light which surrounds the invisible Spirit, and his sparks, and she was impregnated by him. And a

spark of light produced a light resembling his blessedness but it did not equal his greatness. This was the only-begotten child of the Mother-Father which had come forth. It is the only offspring and the only begotten of the Father, the pure Light.

And the invisible, pure, undefiled Spirit rejoiced over the light which was created, that which was produced by the first power of his Thought, which is Barbelo. And he poured his goodness over it until it became perfect and did not lack in any goodness, because he had anointed the child with the goodness of the invisible Spirit. It was his child and the child was there with him and he poured upon the child an anointing. And immediately when the child had received the Spirit, it glorified the Holy Spirit and the perfect Divine Thought, because the child owed these its existence.

And it asked to be given Mind as a fellow worker, and he agreed gladly. And when the invisible Spirit had agreed, the Mind was created, and it attended the anointed one (Christ), glorifying him and Barbelo. And all these were created in silence.

And Mind wanted to initiate an action through the word of the invisible Spirit. Thus, his will became an action and it appeared with the mind; and the light glorified it. And the word followed the will. It was because of the word that Christ, the divine self-created one, created everything. And Eternal Life and his will and Mind and Foreknowledge attended and glorified the invisible Spirit and Barbelo, because of whom they had been created.

And the Holy Spirit perfected and matured the divine Self-created one, and brought the son, together with Barbelo, so that he might present himself to the mighty and invisible, pure, undefiled Spirit as the divine Self-created one, the Christ (the anointed one) who loudly proclaimed honor to the spirit. He was created through Forethought. And the invisible, pure, undefiled Spirit placed the divine Self-created one of truth over everything. And he caused every authority to be subject to him and to Truth, which is in him, so that he may know the name of the "All," whose name is exalted above every name. That name will only be spoken to those who are worthy of it.

From the light, which is the Christ, there is incorruptibleness and through the gift of the Spirit four lights shone from the divine Self-created one. He wished that they might be with him. And the three are will, thought, and life. And the four powers are Understanding, Grace, Perception, and Thoughtfulness.

 And Grace belongs to the everlasting realm of the luminary Harmozel, which is the first angel. And there are three other kingdoms with this everlasting kingdom: Grace, Truth, and Form. And the second luminary is Oriel, who has authority over the second everlasting realm. And there are three other kingdoms with him: Conception, Perception, and Memory. And the third luminary is Daveithai, who has authority over the third everlasting realm. And there are three other kingdoms with him: Understanding, Love, and Idea. And the fourth luminary, Eleleth , was given authority over the fourth everlasting realm. And there are three other kingdoms with him: Perfection, Peace, and Wisdom (Sophia). These are the four luminaries which serve the divine Self-created one. These are the twelve kingdoms which serve the child of god, the Self-created one, the Christ. They serve him through the will and the grace of the invisible Spirit. The twelve kingdoms belong to the child of the Self-created one. All things were established by the will of the Holy Spirit through the Self-created one.

From the Foreknowledge of the perfect mind, through the expression of the will of the invisible Spirit and the will of the Self-created one, the perfect Man came into being. He was the first revelation and the truth. The pure, undefiled Spirit called him "Adam, The Stranger" (not of the earthly realm, but belonging to the divine realm). The spirit placed him over the first realm with the mighty one, the Self-created one, the Christ, by the authority of the first luminary, Harmozel; and with him are his powers. And the invisible one gave Adam The Stranger an invincible spiritual power. And Adam The Stranger spoke, glorifying and praising the invisible Spirit, saying, "It is because of you that everything has been created and therefore, everything will return to you. I shall praise and glorify you and the Self-created one and all the realms, the three: the Father, the Mother, and the Son, who make up the perfect power."

And Adam The Stranger placed his son Seth over the second realm in which the second luminary Oriel is present. And in the third realm the children of Seth were established over the third luminary, Daveithai. And the souls of the saints were lodged there. In the fourth realm the souls are kept of those who do not know the pleroma and who did not repent at once. These are they who persisted for a while and repented afterwards; they are in the area of the fourth luminary, Eleleth. They are those which glorify the invisible Spirit.

And the Sophia of the eternal realm manifested a thought from herself through the invisible Spirit and Foreknowledge. She wanted to produce a likeness of herself out of herself without the consent of the Spirit, but he had not approved. She attempted this act without her male consort, and without his permission. She had no male approval thus, she had not found her agreement. She had considered this without the consent of the

Spirit and the knowledge of her compliment, but she brought forth her creation anyway. Because of the invincible power she possessed her thought did not remain idle, and something came out of her which was imperfect and different from her appearance because she had produced it without her compliment. It did not look like its mother because it has another form.

As she beheld the results of her desire, it changed into a form of a lion-faced serpent. Its eyes were like fire-like lightning which flashed. When she saw it she cast it away from her and threw it outside the realm so that none of the immortal ones might see it, for she had created it in ignorance. She surrounded it with a brightly glowing cloud and she put a throne in the middle of the cloud that no one might see it except the Holy Spirit who is called the mother of all that lives. And she called his name Yaldaboth.

This is the first Archon who took great power from his mother. And he left her and moved away from the realm in which he was born. He became strong and created for himself other kingdoms with a flame of glowing fire which still existed. And he mated with his own mindless ego that he had with him (he masturbated / or he was like his mother and did the same act of creation by himself) and brought into existence authorities for himself.

The name of the first one is Athoth, whom the generations call the reaper.
The second one is Harmas, who is the eye of envy.
The third one is Kalila-Oumbri.
The fourth one is Yabel.
The fifth one is Adonaiou, who is called Sabaoth (fool or chaos).

The sixth one is Cain, whom the generations of humans call the sun.

The seventh is Abel.

The eighth is Abrisene.

The ninth is Yobel.

The tenth is Armoupieel.

The eleventh is Melceir-Adonein.

The twelfth is Belias, it is he who is over the depth of Hades.

(These could be the 12 stations of the zodiac.)

There he placed seven kings corresponding to the sections of heaven to reign over the seven heavens and he placed five to reign over the depth of the abyss. (There were 7 known planets at the time of writing.) And he shared his fire with them, but he did not relinquish any power of the light which he had taken from his mother, for he is ignorant darkness.

And when light is added to darkness, it made the darkness bright. When darkness is added to light, it dims the light and it became neither light nor dark, but it became like dusk.

Now the Archon who is like the gloaming (gloom) has three names. The first name is Yaldaboth (fool / son of chaos), the second is Saklas, and the third is Samael. And he is evil in the arrogance and thoughtlessness that is in him. For he said, "I am God and there is no other God beside me" (Isaiah chapters 45 and 46). He said this because he did not know where his strength originated, nor from where he himself had come.

And the Archons created seven powers for themselves, and the powers created for themselves six angels for each one until they became 365 angels (the number of days in the solar year). And these are the bodies belonging with the names:

The first is Athoth, a he has a sheep's face;

The second is Eloaiou, he has a donkey's face;

The third is Astaphaios, he has a hyena's face;

The fourth is Yao, he has a snake face with seven heads;

The fifth is Sabaoth, he has a dragon's face;

The sixth is Adonin, he has an ape face;

The seventh is Sabbede (or Sabbadaios), he has a face that shone like fire.

This is the nature of seven types within the week.

But Yaldaboth had a plethora of faces, more than all of them, so that he could exhibit any face he wished to any of them, when he is in the midst of seraphim (seraphim plural of seraph. Seraphim are a class or type of angel of which, according to this text, Yaldaboth seems to be the head). He shared his fire with them and became their lord. He called himself God because of the power of the glory (brightness) he possessed that was taken from his mother's light. He rebelled against the place from which he came.

And he united the seven powers of his thoughts with the authorities that were with him. And when he spoke it became (happened).

And he named each power beginning with the highest:

The first is goodness with the first authority, Athoth;

The second is foreknowledge with the second power, Eloaio; The third is divinity with the third one, Astraphaio);

The fourth is lordship with the fourth power, Yao;

The fifth is kingdom with the fifth one, Sabaoth;

The sixth is envy with the sixth one, Adonein;

The seventh is understanding with the seventh one, Sabbateon.

And these each have a kingdom (sphere on influence) within the realm (kingdom of heaven).

They were given names according to the glory belonging to heaven for the powers of their destructiveness. And there was power in the names given to them by their creator. But the names they were given according to the glory of heaven would mean their loss of power and their destruction. Thus they have two names.

He (Yaldaboth) created all things and structured things after the model of the first kingdom created so that he might create things in an incorruptible manner. It was not because he had ever seen the indestructible ones, but the power in him, which he had taken from his mother, produced in him the image of the order of the universe. And when he saw the creation surrounding him the innumerable amount of angels around him that had come from him, he said to them, "I am a jealous God, and there is no other God beside me." (Exodus 20:3) But by announcing this he had let the angels who were with him know that there is another God. If there were no other god, why would he be jealous?

Then the mother began to move here and there. She realized she had lost part of herself when the brightness of her light dimmed. And she became darker because her partner had not consorted with her.

I (John) said, Lord, what does it mean that she moved here and there? The Lord smiled and said, "Do not think it happened the way that Moses said it did 'above the waters'." (Genesis 1:2) No, it did not, but when she had seen the wickedness which had happened, and the fact her son had stolen from her, she repented. In the darkness of ignorance she began to forget and to be ashamed. She did not dare to go back there, but she was restless. This restlessness was the moving here and there.

And the prideful one stole power from his mother. For he was ignorant and thought that there was no other in existence except his mother. When he saw innumerable angels he had created he exalted himself above them. When the mother recognized that the cloak (body) of darkness was imperfect, and she knew that her partner had not consorted with her, she repented and wept greatly. The entire pleroma heard the prayer of her repentance, and they praised the invisible, pure, undefiled Spirit on her behalf. And the Spirit agreed and when he agreed the Holy Spirit anointed her from the entire pleroma. For her consort did not come to her alone, but he brought to her through the pleroma that which was needed to restore what she was lacking. And she was allowed to ascend, not to her own kingdom but to the kingdom above her son, that she could remain in the ninth (heaven / kingdom) until she restored what she lacked in herself.

And a voice called from the highest kingdom of heaven: "The Man exists and the son of Man." And the head Archon, Yaldaboth, heard it and thought that the voice had come from his mother. He did not know whence it came. He taught them, the holy and perfect Mother-Father, the complete Foreknowledge, the image of the invisible one who is the Father of the all things and through whom everything came into being, the first Man. He is the one who revealed his image in human form.

And the whole kingdom of the first (head) Archon quaked, and the foundations of the abyss shook. And the underside of waters, which are above the material world, were illuminated by the appearance of his image which had been revealed. When all the authorities and the head Archon looked, they saw the whole region of the underside (of the waters) that was illuminated. And through the light they saw the form of the image (reflected) in the water.

And he (Yaldaboth) said to the authorities of him, "Come, let us make a man using the image of God as a template to our likeness, that his image may become a light for us." And they created by the means of their various powers matching the features which were given to them. And each authority supplied a feature in the form of the image which Yaldaboth had seen in its natural form. He created a being according to the likeness of the first, perfect Man. And they said, "Let us call him Adam (man), that his name may be a power of light for us."

And the powers began to create.
The first one, Goodness, created a bone essence; and the second, Foreknowledge, created a sinew essence; the third, Divinity, created a flesh essence; and the fourth, the Lordship, created a marrow essence; the fifth, Kingdom created a blood essence; the sixth, Envy, created a skin essence; the seventh, Understanding, created a hair essence. And the multitude of the angels were with him and they received from the powers the seven elements of the natural (form) so they could create the proportions of the limbs and the proportion of the buttocks and correct functioning of each of the parts together.

The first one began to create the head. Eteraphaope-Abron created his head; Meniggesstroeth created the brain; Asterechme created the right eye; Thaspomocha, the left eye; Yeronumos, the right ear; Bissoum, the left ear; Akioreim, the nose; Banen-Ephroum, the lips; Amen, the teeth; Ibikan, the molars; Basiliademe, the tonsils; Achcha, the uvula; Adaban, the neck; Chaaman, the vertebrae; Dearcho, the throat; Tebar, the right shoulder; the left shoulder; Mniarcon, the right elbow; the left elbow;

Abitrion, the right underarm; Evanthen, the left underarm; Krys, the right
hand; Beluai, the left hand; Treneu, the fingers of the right hand; Balbel,
the fingers of the left hand; Kriman, the nails of the hands; Astrops, the
right breast; Barroph, the left breast; Baoum, the right shoulder joint;
Ararim, the left shoulder joint; Areche, the belly; Phthave, the navel;
Senaphim, the abdomen; Arachethopi, the right ribs; Zabedo, the left ribs;
Barias, the right hip; Phnouth the left hip; Abenlenarchei, the marrow;
Chnoumeninorin, the bones; Gesole, the stomach; Agromauna, the heart;
Bano, the lungs; Sostrapal, the liver; Anesimalar, the spleen; Thopithro,
the intestines; Biblo, the kidneys; Roeror, the sinews; Taphreo, the spine
of the body; Ipouspoboba, the veins; Bineborin, the arteries;
Atoimenpsephei, theirs are the breaths which are in all the limbs;
Entholleia, all the flesh; Bedouk, the right buttock; Arabeei, the penis;
Eilo, the testicles; Sorma, the genitals; Gorma-Kaiochlabar, the right
thigh; Nebrith, the left thigh; Pserem, the kidneys of the right leg;
Asaklas, the left kidney; Ormaoth, the right leg; Emenun, the left leg;
Knyx, the right shin-bone; Tupelon, the left shin-bone; Achiel, the right
knee; Phnene, the left knee; Phiouthrom, the right foot; Boabel, its toes;
Trachoun, the left foot; Phikna, its toes; Miamai, the nails of the feet;
Labernioum.

And those who were appointed over all of these are: Zathoth, Armas,
Kalila, Jabel, (Sabaoth, Cain, Abel). And those who are particularly active
in the limbs are the head Diolimodraza, the neck Yammeax, the right
shoulder Yakouib, the left shoulder Verton, the right hand Oudidi, the
left one Arbao, the fingers of the right hand Lampno, the fingers of the
left hand Leekaphar, the right breast Barbar, the left breast Imae, the chest
Pisandriaptes, the right shoulder joint Koade, the left shoulder joint
Odeor, the right ribs Asphixix, the left ribs Synogchouta, the belly
Arouph, the womb Sabalo, the right thigh Charcharb, the left thigh

Chthaon, all the genitals Bathinoth, the right leg Choux, the left leg Charcha, the right shin-bone Aroer, the left shin-bone Toechtha, the right knee Aol, the left knee Charaner, the right foot Bastan, its toes Archentechtha, the left foot Marephnounth, its toes Abrana.

(Note: Could this be those constructing human DNA or the blueprint to the human form? Were we created as an experiment of another race?)

Seven have power over all of these: Michael, Ouriel, Asmenedas, Saphasatoel, Aarmouriam, Richram, Amiorps. And the ones who are in charge of the senses are Archendekta; and he who is in charge of the receptions is Deitharbathas; and he who is in charge over the imagination is Oummaa; and he who is over creativity Aachiaram, and he who is over the whole impulse Riaramnacho.

The origin of the demons that are in the entire body is known to be these four: heat, cold, wetness, and dryness. And the mother of all of them is the material creation. And he who rules over the heat is Phloxopha; and he who rules over the cold is Oroorrothos; and he who rules over what is dry is Erimacho; and he who rules over the wetness is Athuro. And the mother of all of these is Onorthochrasaei, who stands in with them without limits, and she coverts with all of them. She is truly material and they are sustained by her.

The four ruling demons are: Ephememphi, who is attached to pleasure,
Yoko, who is attached to desire,
Nenentophni, who is attached to grief,
Blaomen, who is attached to fear,
and the mother of them all is Aesthesis-Ouch-Epi-Ptoe.
And from the four demons passions were created. And grief spawned

envy, jealousy, distress, trouble, pain, callousness, anxiety, mourning, and more. Pleasure spawned wickedness, vanity, pride, and similar things. Desire spawned anger, wrath, and bitterness, and driving passion, the inability to be satisfied, and similar things. Fear spawned dread, subservience, agony, and shame. These are both good and evil, but the understanding of their nature is attributed to Anaro, who is over the material soul. It belongs with the seven senses, which are controlled by Ouch-Epi-Ptoe.

This is the number of the angels: together they are 365. They all worked on it from limb to limb, until the physical (material) body was completed by them. Now there are other ones in charge over the remaining passions whom I did not mention to you. But if you wish to know them, it is written in the book of Zoroaster. And all the angels and demons worked until they had constructed (fashioned) the physical body. And their creation was completely devoid of activity and was motionless for a long time.

And when the mother (Sophia) wanted to recapture the power which was taken from her by the head Archon, she prayed to the Mother-Father of the All, who is most merciful. He sent a holy decree containing the five lights down to the place where the angels of the head Archon reside. They advised him (Yaldaboth) that he should bring forth the power of the mother. And they said to Yaldaboth, "Blow some of your spirit into his face and his body will arise." And he blew the spirit power of the mother into his (Adam's) face. (Genesis 2:7) Yaldaboth did not know to do this because he existed in ignorance. And the power of the mother went out of Yaldaboth into Adam's physical body, which they had fashioned after the image of the one who exists from the beginning. The body moved and

gained strength, and it was enlightened.

(See "The Gnostic Scriptures", published by Fifth Estate)

Are we being told in this story that the creation and attempted destruction of man was a war between teams of beings? Was our creation parsed out, as it would be in a science lab?

We see that there is more information given regarding Angels and Demons in the Gnostic writings, including their names and practices. The story of angel, demon, God, and man is a complex one, and one that may lead us from myth into realties we may not wish to go.

By contrasting and comparing ancient texts containing angels, demons, and man; a full and panoramic history is produced. In this history the startling revelation of the descent of man and angels, and the evolution of evil on earth is clearly revealed.

The books selected for this purpose are, The First and Second Books of Adam and Eve, The First and Second Books of Enoch, The Book of Jubilees, The Book of Jasher, The War Scrolls, The Book of the Giants, and The Bible. Each of these ancient texts carries within it a piece of the story. By weaving the stories together, the origins of angels and demons are brought into focus.

Related scriptures are interwoven to add detail to the history of spiritual beings. In these cases scriptures may be inserted non-chronologically. However, these are digressions used to emphasize certain points within the ancient texts.

Certain familiar Jewish oral traditions and myths were inserted at the appropriate places in the timeline. Since myths are given less weight of authenticity, the passages are included in italics to distinguish them from the more accepted texts.

Although there were fragments from over 600 separate scrolls found in the caves of Qumran, only a few fragments were used in tracing the history of evil. The Dead Sea Scrolls comprise documents, including texts from the Hebrew Bible, discovered between 1947 and 1956 in eleven caves in and around the Wadi Qumran on the northwest shore of the Dead Sea. They are Biblical and religious documents of great historical value dating from before AD 200.

No story is complete without a resolution to the problem. Essene literature sees the conclusion in the person of the "teacher of righteousness." This figure was the Messiah who would come to teach and guide them into the new kingdom. This figure is fulfilled in the person of Jesus as he establishes his eternal kingdom at his second coming. Thus, the story of angels and demons and man's conquest over Satan or Mastema ends when he is overcome and destroyed by the teacher of righteousness, Jesus, the Messiah. The story presented here is an abbreviated one drawn from the New Testament books of Matthew, Mark, Luke, John, Acts, and Revelation.

From the beginning of man's oral history, through our present age, and ending with prophecies some say will occur in this generation, the story is told. Its origin and its conclusion are laid out before us in the words of historians, priests, and prophets, to be read as a warning of our own susceptibility to enemies unseen. But, where did the idea of angels and demons originate?

In what most would consider a "normal" and "rational" world, angels and demons cannot be seen, touched, or heard. If they exist at all, they would spiritual beings cloaked from our senses, with purposes known only to themselves and the source of their assignments. God assigns tasks to angels and Satan directs demons. So, how did we, as a worldwide race of people, come to believe there were such creatures?

One theory has to do with the evolution of religion itself. Ancient religions tended to be polytheistic with gods having dominion over certain areas of nature or human activities such as weather, harvest, hunting, or procreation. Other deities accounted for the violence in the world and were malevolent in nature.

In the area of Egypt there were dozens of such deities. To prove a point, a partial list is included in Appendix "A":

This is only a partial list, representing some of the gods thought responsible for directing the outcome of daily human activity. Some gods and goddesses were thought to be naturally good and predisposed to helping man in his affairs, while others were thought to be destructive by nature and responsible for death and despair.

Underneath it all was the thought that good and evil could not originate from the same source. A loving and gracious deity could not be the same deity that would kill a wife, mother, or even an unborn child. The primitive mind could not conceive of such a thing. Modern man is not much different.

As the pantheon of gods shrank and evolved, certain religions, such as the Zoroastrians, settled into a duality of gods, or as the modern Abrahamic faiths of Judaism, Islam, and Christianity present it, a monotheistic religion with an adversary.

In its oldest form, Judaism was a combination of Canaanite and Jewish religions, as each influenced the other. Yet, even as Judaism strained to be free of Canaanite polytheism, it could not be completely free, as the previous verse in Psalms on page 28 indicates.

There is also a passage from Jewish midrash in which Hannah is praying for a child at Shiloh: "Lord of the Universe! The heavenlys never die, and they do not reproduce their kind. Terrestrial beings die, but they are fruitful and multiply. Therefore I pray: Either make me immortal, or give me a son!"

Why do we find references to evil in religions that hold to a single good God who created everything? Why is there a need for messengers, called angels, to do the will of an all powerful and omniscient God? It is because no religion stands alone. None is pure. All religions evolve and borrow from previous faiths, and none can reconcile absolute good and absolute evil emanating from the same god.

Zoroastrianism has so influenced major religions that many of its concepts have been integrated and thought to be native to the other faiths, such as heaven and hell, God and the evil adversary ahriman, the coming of the Saviour or Saoshyant born of a virgin, the end-time cleansing of the world by fire, the resurrection of the dead (Ristakhiz), the creation of a new world (Frashogard) and even the final battle between good and evil. These beliefs filtered down to Judaism during the reign of King Khushru (Cyrus) of Iran. From Judaism the beliefs were propagated to Christianity and Islam.

Why must there be an adversary? Again, we are back to the problem of attempting to justify a single source of good and evil within our limited minds. Even if God created the source of evil, the free will dispensed from God to the being frees God from full culpability of the evil acts perpetrated by his creation. (Even though some argue that angels, and thus Satan, were created without free will.)

Could it be that the existence of Satan and his demons are simply a coping mechanism for the monotheistic faiths, or is there a personification of evil in the form of a malevolent entity? Did this entity persuade part of a spiritual army of beings to follow him? Was there an uprising of evil in heaven that attempted to overthrow God himself?

Angel and demons: Are they the dying echoes of polytheism, or the servants and enemies for the one true God?

If we compare the list of gods and their domains to a list of angels, we can see a parallel of characteristics in various religious traditions. Found in Appendix "B" is a list of angels and demons from various religions and myths throughout the world. Each has a name and a purpose or power, much like the ancient gods of our polytheistic past.

Many of the religions that first taught the existence of divine messengers and servants of god were polytheistic. They did not have the impetus or necessity to divest a single god of benevolent or evil attributes. The mention of angels and demons can be traced to religions that are not monotheistic, existing earlier than monotheism. Thus, we are stuck in this circular logic begging the question: "Are angels and demons the invention of the primitive mind, which envisioned a pantheon of gods and their servants, involved in petty and emotional squabbles, like those old gods of Rome? Are angels and demons a throw-back to paganism used to distance a singular God from evil results of his primal causality of creation, or, are they real?" Do angels and demons exist? If they do, are they who and what we have been taught they are? Some ancient texts tell us exactly what the fallen angel, called the Watchers, taught mankind.

First, let us do a quick examination of the ancient text of Enoch. (The Lost Book of Enoch). We are told that 200 beings called "The Watchers" made a pact between themselves to descend en mass to earth and copulate with the women they had seen and chosen. The pact was thought to protect each one from committing to the evil act alone. It appears they thought that mutual culpability would lessen the crime or punishment.

These were "spiritual beings." After they succeeded in their corporeal deed they did not return to their posts. We are told in the text of their contribution to the knowledge base of humanity. The Watchers lived among mankind, teaching arts of writing, metalworking, potions, the use of herbs, and more. They lived with their wives and changed the complexion of mankind forever. Their offspring became what the Bible calls, "the men of renown. These were the heroes of old; those beings of myth and legend, who were more than mere mortals. Some offspring were those old giants, monsters and man-eaters of myth.

The Fall of The Watchers
From "The Lost Book of Enoch", published by Fifth Estate.

Lost Book of Enoch
[Chapter 6]

1 And it came to pass when the children of men had multiplied that in those days were born to them beautiful and fair daughters.

GEN 6:1 And it came to pass, when men began to multiply on the face of the earth, and daughters were born unto them, 2 That the sons of God saw the daughters of men that they were fair; and they took them wives of all which they chose. 3 And the LORD said, My spirit shall not always strive with man, for that he also is flesh: yet his days shall be an hundred and twenty years.

2 And the angels, the sons of heaven, saw and lusted after them, and said to one another: 'Come, let us choose us wives from among the children of men

.

3 And have children with them.' And Semjaza, who was their leader, said to them: 'I fear you will not agree to do this deed,

4 And I alone shall have to pay the penalty of this great sin.'

5 And they all answered him and said: 'Let us all swear an oath, and all bind ourselves by mutual curses so we will not abandon this plan but to do this

thing.' Then they all swore together and bound themselves by mutual curses.

6 And they were in all two hundred who descended in the days of Jared in the summit of Mount Hermon, and they called it Mount Hermon, because they had sworn and bound themselves by mutual curses on the act.

JUDE 1:5 I will therefore put you in remembrance, though ye once knew this, how that the Lord, having saved the people out of the land of Egypt, afterward destroyed them that believed not. 6 And the angels who kept not their first estate, but left their own habitation, he hath reserved in everlasting chains under darkness unto the judgment of the great day.

7 And these are the names of their leaders: Samlazaz, their leader, Araklba, Rameel, Kokablel, Tamlel, Ramlel, Danel, Ezeqeel, Baraqijal,

(Author's note: Samlazaz could be another spelling of Semjaza, and possibly be the same entity.)

8 Asael, Armaros, Batarel, Ananel, Zaqiel, Samsapeel, Satarel, Turel, Jomjael, Sariel. These are their chiefs of tens.

[Chapter 7]

1 And all of them together went and took wives for themselves, each choosing one for himself, and they began to go in to them and to defile themselves with sex with them,

GEN 5:32 And Noah was five hundred years old: and Noah begat Shem, Ham, and Japheth. 6:1 And it came to pass, when men began to multiply on the face of the

earth, and daughters were born unto them, 2   That the sons of God saw the daughters of men that they were fair; and they took them wives of all which they chose. 3 And the LORD said, My spirit shall not always strive with man, for that he also is flesh: yet his days shall be an hundred and twenty years. 4 There were giants in the earth in those days; and also after that, when the sons of God came in unto the daughters of men, and they bare children to them, the same became mighty men which were of old, men of renown. 5 And GOD saw that the wickedness of man was great in the earth, and that every imagination of the thoughts of his heart was only evil continually. 6 And it repented the LORD that he had made man on the earth, and it grieved him at his heart.

2 And the angels taught them charms and spells, and the cutting of roots, and made them acquainted with plants.

3 And the women became pregnant, and they bare large giants, whose height was three thousand cubits (ells).

4 The giants consumed all the work and toil of men. And when men could no longer sustain them, the giants turned against them and devoured mankind.

5 And they began to sin against birds, and beasts, and reptiles, and fish, and to devour one another's flesh, and drank the blood.

6 Then the earth laid accusation against the lawless ones.

[Chapter 8]

1 And Azazel taught men to make swords, and knives, and shields, and breastplates, and taught them about metals of the earth and the art of working them, and bracelets, and ornaments, and the use of antimony, and the beautifying of the eyelids, and all kinds of precious stones, and all coloring and dyes.

2 And there was great impiety, they turned away from God, and committed fornication, and they were led astray, and became corrupt in all their ways.

3 Semjaza taught the casting of spells, and root-cuttings, Armaros taught counter-spells (release from spells), Baraqijal taught astrology, Kokabel taught the constellations (portents), Ezeqeel the knowledge of the clouds, Araqiel the signs of the earth, Shamsiel the signs of the sun, and Sariel the course of the moon. And as men perished, they cried, and their cry went up to heaven.

[Chapter 9]

1 And then Michael, Uriel, Raphael, and Gabriel looked down from heaven and saw much blood being shed on the earth, and all lawlessness being done on the earth.

2 And they said to each other: 'Let the cries from the destruction of Earth ascend up to the gates of heaven.

3 And now to you, the holy ones of heaven, the souls of men make their petition, saying, "Bring our cause before the Most High."'

4 And they said to the Lord of the ages: 'Lord of lords, God of gods, King of kings, and God of the ages, the throne of your glory endures through all the

generations of the ages, and your name is holy and glorious and blessed to all the ages!

1TI 6:15 Which in his times he shall shew, who is the blessed and only Potentate, the King of kings, and Lord of lords; 16 Who only hath immortality, dwelling in the light which no man can approach unto; whom no man hath seen, nor can see: to whom be honour and power everlasting. Amen.

5 You have made all things, and you have power over all things: and all things are revealed and open in your sight, and you see all things, and nothing can hide itself from you.

6 Look at what Azazel has done, who hath taught all unrighteousness on earth and revealed the eternal secrets which were made and kept in heaven, which men were striving to learn:

7 And Semjaza, who taught spells, to whom you gave authority to rule over his associates.

8 And they have gone to the daughters of men on the earth, and have had sex with the women, and have defiled themselves, and revealed to them all kinds of sins.

GEN 6:4 There were giants in the earth in those days; and also after that, when the sons of God came in unto the daughters of men, and they bare children to them, the same became mighty men which were of old, men of renown.

9 And the women have borne giants, and the whole earth has thereby been filled with blood and unrighteousness.

GEN 6:5 And GOD saw that the wickedness of man was great in the earth, and that every imagination of the thoughts of his heart was only evil continually. 6 And it repented the LORD that he had made man on the earth, and it grieved him at his heart.

10 And now, behold, the souls of those who have died are crying out and making their petition to the gates of heaven, and their lament has ascended and cannot cease because of the lawless deeds which are done on the earth.

11 And you know all things before they come to pass, and you see these things and you have permitted them, and say nothing to us about these things. What are we to do with them about these things?'

[Chapter 10]

1 Then said the Most High, the Great and Holy One, Uriel go to the son of Lamech.

2 Say to him: 'Go to Noah and tell him in my name "Hide yourself!" and reveal to him the end that is approaching: that the whole earth will be destroyed, and a flood is about to come on the whole earth, and will destroy everything on it.'

GEN 7:4 For yet seven days, and I will cause it to rain upon the earth forty days and forty nights; and every living substance that I have made will I destroy from off the face of the earth.

3 'And now instruct him as to what he must do to escape that his offspring may be preserved for all the generations of the world.'

GEN 6:13 And God said unto Noah, The end of all flesh is come before me; for the earth is filled with violence through them; and, behold, I will destroy them with the earth. 14 Make thee an ark of gopher wood; rooms shalt thou make in the ark, and shalt pitch it within and without with pitch.

4 And again the Lord said to Raphael: 'Bind Azazel hand and foot, and cast him into the darkness and split open the desert, which is in Dudael, and cast him in.

5 And fill the hole by covering him with rough and jagged rocks, and cover him with darkness, and let him live there for ever, and cover his face that he may not see the light.

6 And on the day of the great judgment he shall be hurled into the fire.

7 And heal the earth which the angels have ruined, and proclaim the healing of the earth, for I will restore the earth and heal the plague, that not all of the children of men may perish through all the secret things that the Watchers have disclosed and have taught their sons.

ROM 8:18 For I reckon that the sufferings of this present time are not worthy to be compared with the glory which shall be revealed in us. 19 For the earnest expectation of the creature waiteth for the manifestation of the sons of God. 20 For the creature was made subject to vanity, not willingly, but by reason of him who hath subjected the same in hope, 21 Because the creature itself also shall be delivered from the bondage of corruption into the glorious liberty of the children of God.

8 The whole earth has been corrupted through the works that were taught by Azazel: to him ascribe ALL SIN.'

9 To Gabriel said the Lord: 'Proceed against the bastards and the reprobates, and against the children of fornication and destroy the children of fornication and the children of the Watchers. Cause them to go against one another that they may destroy each other in battle: Shorten their days.

GEN 6:7 And the LORD said, I will destroy man whom I have created from the face of the earth; both man, and beast, and the creeping thing, and the fowls of the air; for it repenteth me that I have made them. 8 But Noah found grace in the eyes of the LORD.

10 No request that (the Watchers) their fathers make of you shall be granted them on their behalf; for they hope to live an eternal life, and that each one of them will live five hundred years.'

11 And the Lord said to Michael: 'Go, bind Semjaza and his team who have associated with women and have defiled themselves in all their uncleanness.

12 When their sons have slain one another, and they have seen the destruction of their beloved ones, bind them fast for seventy generations under the hills of the earth, until the day of the consummation of their judgment and until the eternal judgment is accomplished.

(Author's note: 70 generations of 500 years = 3500 years.)

13 In those days they shall be led off to the abyss of fire and to the torment and the prison in which they shall be confined for ever.'

14 Then Semjaza shall be burnt up with the condemned and they will be destroyed, having been bound together with them to the end of all generations.

15 Destroy all the spirits of lust and the children of the Watchers, because they have wronged mankind.

16 Destroy all wrong from the face of the earth and let every evil work come to an end and let (the earth be planted with righteousness) the plant of righteousness and truth appear; and it shall prove a blessing, the works of righteousness and truth shall be planted in truth and joy for evermore.

GEN 6:7 And the LORD said, I will destroy man whom I have created from the face of the earth; both man, and beast, and the creeping thing, and the fowls of the air; for it repenteth me that I have made them.

17 And then shall all the righteous survive, and shall live until they beget thousands of children, and all the days of their youth and their old age shall they complete in peace.

GEN 8:22 While the earth remaineth, seedtime and harvest, and cold and heat, and summer and winter, and day and night shall not cease.

GEN 9:1 And God blessed Noah and his sons, and said unto them, Be fruitful, and multiply, and replenish the earth.

18 And then shall the whole earth be untilled in righteousness and shall be planted with trees and be full of blessing. And all desirable trees shall be planted on it, and they shall plant vines on it.

19 And the vine which they plant shall yield fruit in abundance, and as for all the seed which is sown, each measurement (of it) shall bear a thousand, and each measurement of olives shall yield ten presses of oil.

20 You shall cleanse the earth from all oppression, and from all unrighteousness, and from all sin, and from all godlessness, and all the uncleanness that is brought on the earth you shall destroy from off the earth.

21 All the children of men shall become righteous, and all nations shall offer adoration and shall praise Me,

22 And all shall worship Me. And the earth shall be cleansed from all defilement, and from all sin, and from all punishment, and from all torment, and I will never again send another flood from this generation to all generations and for ever.

Genesis 6

1 When men began to increase in number on the earth and daughters were born to them, 2 the sons of God saw that the daughters of men were beautiful, and they married any of them they chose. 3 Then the LORD said, "My Spirit will not contend with man forever, for he is mortal; his days will be a hundred and twenty years."
4 The Nephilim were on the earth in those days — and also afterward — when the sons of God went to the daughters of men and had children by them. They were the heroes of old, men of renown.

(The word "Nephilim" means "The Fallen.")

Why did the watchers stay? Did they form an attachment to the women? Did they love them, or were they simply trapped on earth. These spiritual beings did not need to stay. They could have left to conquer other females. They could have waged war on man and ruled over them. Instead, they stayed and taught. It could have been possible for them to returned to heaven, yet there is a hint in the text that suggests they were changed by the union and became "defiled" and possibly unable to return to their prior purely spiritual state and were thus trapped in the physical realm.

The oldest books speak to the fact that the sprits and bodies detached during death. There was no place created for the souls of these hybrid demons. The spirits were released into the world to roam and destroy, unseen and undetectable, like the succubus, stealing life from babies and oppressing the souls of men. They inhabited the bodies of animals and roamed about seeking human victims to spiritually feed on. These are the demons of our myths, our bible, and of our darkest fears. But, the fathers of the demons were the Watchers – angels in human form with extraordinary powers. These were the heroes, titans, and men of legend. These theories are summed up in the Book of Giants.

The Book of Giants

The patriarch Enoch is well known to readers of the Bible. The Bible declares his age to be 365 years, at which time it was said he did not die but he simply "walked with God" and afterward "he was not, because God had taken him" (Gen. 5:24). Many books have been written about Enoch. The oldest of these is known simply as The Book of Enoch, which is explained in full later in this book. Along with "The Second

Book of Enoch" they form an important source for what has come to be known as Enochian literature. There are also other less known books, such as The Third Book of Enoch. In all, there are five books of varying value in the Enochian literature.

During the excavation of the caves of Qumran parts of all but one of the five major components of the Ethiopic anthology have been found along with an additional unknown texts called, "The Book of Giants."

According to The Book of Enoch and the Book of Giants, 200 angels, called Watchers pledged an oath to go down together to do sexual deeds. The Book of Enoch tells us that the offspring of these unnatural unions were giants, nephilim, and eljo, although we have no information on what an eljo is, we know that the word "nephilim" means "the fallen ones." The angels, known as the Watchers began to teach humans to do evil, using spells and charms. Their offspring were born evil and enraged, committing sin continually. For this reason God determined to imprison the angels until the final judgment and to destroy the earth with a flood. The Book of Giants expands and elaborates on the narrative of the giants, especially the two children of Shemihaza, one of the head Watchers.

For those who have considered the connections between the Greek, Roman, and Babylonian myths of gods, heroes, titans, and monsters, this codex is quite interesting. The text forms a bridge and signpost between the stories of the fallen angels and the mythic heroes, monsters and gods of the past, linking one of the Watchers directly to the Babylonian mythic hero, Gilgamesh.

In the text angels and humans interacted. Angels took great liberties with not only women but animals and birds. The intercourse between angels and human women is reported in Genesis (6:1-4), but other stories view this as the beginning of a deeper, spiritual evil on earth. The monsters produced by the unholy copulation between Watchers and animals answers the question of the existence of Centaurs,

Minotaurs, and other monsters, who are half human and half animal. These were produced because the Watchers had taken on human form before breeding with women and animals. God saw this as one of the ultimate abominations. For this reason the great flood was necessary to cleanse the earth. (Compare Gen 6:1 – 4)

The manuscript of the Giants is broken and fragmented. Much of its contents remain a matter of guesswork. Indeed, to make sense of some of the manuscript words or phrases had to be inserted on a "best guess" bais. These words, which are missing from the original fragmented text, are placed within square brackets [].

Most of the content of the present fragments concern dreams regarding the giants and Enoch's attempt to interpret them. Little more than dust remains of the part of the text concerning the giants. Based on the fact that the name of one of the giants is Gilgamesh we can assume that there was some "crosspollination" between The Book of Giants and the ancient Near Eastern mythic epic. The name of one of the angels being the same as the Babylonian hero adds weight to the theory that the titans, heroes, and demigods of old are the fallen angels or their offspring. One must decide whether the epic story influenced this Book of Giants or if the Watchers were in fact the men of renown, as the Bible states.

The dates of the separate documents and events only add to the confusion. The Babylonian epic was written in the third millennium B.C.E. To place the time of the flood one should note that fragments of the Babylonian flood story were found in excavations at Megiddo and dated to around the fourteenth century B.C.E. So the legend of the Great Flood was already established in the Middle East long before Gilgamesh, the Israelite kingdom, or the Bible.

1 [...]

2[. . .] they knew the secrets of [the angels]

3[and] sin was great in the earth [. . .]

4[and there were the Watchers] and they killed man [and took to themselves the daughters of men] 5[. . . they begat] giants [. . .] The angels exploit (consumed) the fruits (fruitfulness) of the earth (consumed all the foods of the earth.)

[... and everything that the] earth produced [...] [...] the great fish [. . .] 14[. . .] the sky with all that grew [. . .] 15[. . . fruit of] the earth and all kinds of grain and all the trees [and their fruits.] 16[. . .] beasts and reptiles . . . [all creeping things of the earth and they observed all [uncleanness]

8[And they preformed every harsh deed and [blasphemous] utterance [. . .] 19[and sexual deeds on] male and female, and among humans [and on animals.]

Note: The two hundred angels chose animals on which to perform unnatural acts on men, women, and animals.

1 [. . . two hundred] 2 donkeys, two hundred asses, two hundred . . . rams of the] 3 flock, two hundred goats, two hundred [. . . beast of the] 4 field from every animal, from every [bird . . .] 5[. . .] for sexual acts regardless of species [. . .] The outcome of the demonic corruption was violence, perversion, and a brood of monstrous beings.

[. . .] they defiled [themselves] 2[. . . they begot] giants and monsters [. . .] 3[. . .] they begot, and, behold, all [the earth was corrupted . . .] 4[. . .] with its blood and by the hand of [the angels. And there was sin and death committed by the offspring of the angels, which are giants. .And the giants began to devour the animals.] 5[giant's] which did not suffice for them and

[. . .] 6[. . .] and they were seeking to devour many [humans...] 7[. . .] 8[and when an animal was offered] the monsters attacked it.

2[Monsters defiled all] flesh [. . .] 3 all [. . .] monsters [. . .] will be [. . .] 4[There were offspring of the monsters and] they would arise [. . .] lacking in true knowledge [. . .] because [. . .] 5[. . .] the earth [grew corrupt . . .] mighty [. . .] 6[. . .] they were considering [. . .] 7[. . .] from the angels upon [. . .] 8[. . .] in the end it will perish and die [. . .] 9[. . .] they caused great corruption in the [earth . . .] [. . . this did not] suffice to [. . .] "they will be [. . .]

Note: The giants begin to be troubled by a series of dreams and visions. Mahway, the titan son of the angel Barakel, reports the first of these dreams to his fellow giants. He sees a tablet being immersed in water. When it emerges, all but three names have been washed away. The dream evidently symbolizes the destruction of all but Noah and his sons by the Flood.

[And one of the giants dreamed a dream...] they drenched the tablet in the water . . .] 2[. . .] the waters went up over the [tablet . . .] 3[. . .] they lifted out the tablet from the water of [. . .] The giant goes to the others and they discuss the dream.

1[. . . this vision] is for cursing and sorrow. I am the one who confessed 2[. . .] the whole group of the castaways that I shall go to [. . .] 3[. . . the spirits of the slain complaining about their killers and crying out 4[. . .] that we shall die together and be made an end of [. . .] much and I will be sleeping, and bread 6[. . .] for my dwelling; the vision and also [. . .] entered into the gathering of the giants 8[. . .]

1 [. . .] Ohya and he said to Mahway [. . .] 2[. . .] without trembling. Who showed you all this vision, [my] brother? 3[. . .] Barakel, my father, was with me. 4[. . .] Before Mahway had finished telling what [he had seen . . .] 5[. . . said] to him, Now I have heard wonders! If a barren woman gives birth [. . .]

[the sons of Shemihaza were Ohya and Hahya.] 3[There] upon Ohya said to Hahya . . .] 4[. . . to be destroyed] from upon the earth and [. . .] 5[. . . the earth. When 6[. . .] they wept before [the giants . . .]

3[. . .] your strength [. . .] 4[. . .] 5 Thereupon Ohya [said] to Hahya [. . .] Then he answered, It is not for us, but for Azaiel, 6 for he did [. . . the children of] angels 7 are the giants, and they would not let all their loved ones] be neglected [. . . we have] not been cast down; you have strength [. . .]

3[. . .] I am a giant, and by the mighty strength of my arm and my own great strength 4 [I can defeat] anyone mortal, and I have made war against them; but I am not [strong enough for our heavenly opponent or to be] able to stand against them, for my opponents 6[. . .] reside in Heaven, and they dwell in the holy places. And not 7[on the earth and they] are stronger than I. 8[. . .] of the wild beast has come, and the wild man they call me. 9[. . .] Then Ohya said to him, I have been forced to have a dream [. . .] the sleep of my eyes vanished in order to let me see a vision. Now I know that on [. . .] 11-12[. . .] Gilgamesh [. . .]

Note: *The first speaker may be Gilgamesh. He has realized the futility of warring against the forces of heaven.*

1 three of its roots [. . .] [while] I was [watching,] there came [. . . they moved the roots into] 3 this garden, all of them, and not [. . .]

Note: Ohya's dream vision is of a tree that is uprooted except for three of its roots; the vision's primary meaning is the same as that of the first dream.

1 concerns the death of our souls [. . .] and all his comrades, and Ohya told them what Gilgamesh said to him 2[. . .] and it was said [. . .] "concerning [. . .] the leader has cursed the authorities and rulers" 3 and the giants were glad at his words. Then he turned and left [. . .]

Note: Ohya tries to avoid the implications of the visions. Above he stated that it referred only to the demon Azazel; here he suggests that the destruction is for the earthly rulers alone.

4 and the sleep of their eye fled from them, and they arose and came to [. . . and told] their dreams, and said in the assembly of their peers, the monsters 6[. . . In] my dream I was watching this very night 7[and there was a garden, and in it were] gardeners and they were watering 8[. . . two hundred trees and] large shoots came out of their root 9[. . .] all the water, and the fire burned all 10[the garden . . .] They found the giants to tell them 11[the dream . . .]

Note: More dreams afflict the giants. The details of this vision are obscure, but it does not bode well for the giants. The dreamers speak first to the monsters, then to the giants. Two of them have had visions or dreams.

Note: Someone suggests that Enoch be found to interpret the vision.

[Go to Enoch,] the noted scribe, and he will interpret for us 12 the dream.

Thereupon his fellow Ohya declared and said to the giants, 13 I too had a dream this night, O giants, and, behold, the Ruler of Heaven came down to earth 14[and destroyed all of us] and such is the end of the dream. [Thereupon] all the giants [and monsters! grew afraid 15 and called Mahway. He came to them and the giants pleaded with him and sent him to Enoch 16[the noted scribe]. They said to him, Go [. . .] to you that 17[. . .] you have heard his voice. And he said to him, He will [. . . and] interpret the dreams [. . .] [and he will tell you] how long the giants have to live. [. . .]

Note: After a journey through time and space, Mahway comes to Enoch and makes his request.

[. . . he soared up in the air] 4 like strong winds, and flew with his hands (flapping) like eagles . . . he left behind] 5 the inhabited world and passed over Desolation, the great desert [and he found Enoch] 6 and Enoch saw him and hailed him, and Mahway said to him [and he yelled] 7 here and there a second time to Mahway [and Mahway said] . . . The giants await 8 your words, and all the monsters of the earth. If [. . .] has been carried [. . .] 9 from the days of [. . .] their [. . .] and they will be added [. . .] 10[regarding the dreams and visions,] we would know from you their meaning [. . .]11[In one of the visions] two hundred trees that from heaven [came down. . .]

1 three of its roots [. . .] [while] I was [watching,] there came [. . . they moved the roots into] 3 this garden, all of them, and not [. . .]

Note: Enoch sends back a tablet with its grim message of judgment, but with hope for repentance.

1 The scribe [Enoch . . .] 2[. . .] 3 a copy of the second tablet that Enoch sent

[. . .] 4 in the very handwriting of Enoch the noted scribe [. . .] In the name of God the great 5 and holy one, to Shemihaza and all [his companions . . .] 6 let it be known to you that not [one of you will be left] 7 and the things you have done, and that your wives [. . .] 8 they and their sons and the wives of [their sons . . .] 9 by your licentiousness on the earth, and there has been upon you [. . . and the land is crying out] 10 and complaining about you and the deeds of your children [. . .] 11 the harm that you have done to it. [. . .] 12 until Raphael arrives, behold, destruction [is coming,in the form a great flood, and it will destroy all living things] 13 and whatever is in the deserts and the seas. And the meaning of the matter [is that judgement is] 14 upon you for evil. But now, loosen the bonds binding you to evil . [repent] l5 and pray.

Note: This fragment details a vision that Enoch saw.

3[. . . great fear] seized me and I fell on my face; I heard his voice [. . .] 4[. . .] he dwelt among human beings but he did not learn from them [. . .]

The Alpha

The origins of evil are planted deeply within each of us. Evil is innocent as a child and monstrously vicious. It feeds upon the same flesh and breathes the same air as saint and martyr. Free will and personal choice direct our steps to heaven or hell and mark us as good or evil. Whether we are Angel, Demon, Watcher, Nephilim, or man, evil is a choice many give themselves over to, fully and completely.

What is evil? Could it be as simple as pernicious selfishness? Could it be the drive for immediate gratification without regard for others? Man's life is limited; one hundred years or less. But, the souls of Angels, Demons, Nephilim, and Watchers are eternal. Consider how much evil can be wrought through millennia of immediate gratification on an eternal scale.

It continues to be pride that keeps us from seeing the truth of our own nature. Pride itself blinds us to our own pride. Pride, arrogance, and selfishness are the seeds and flowers arising from the same root of evil. Evil is the manifestation of the same, all too common, human condition; a condition afflicting angels and demons alike.

"The fear of the Lord is to hate evil: pride, and arrogance, and the evil way, and the froward mouth, do I hate." Proverbs 8:13

The root and cause of all evil arises from a self-centered viewpoint that takes no one else into consideration. It is the drive to control, dominate, and consume. The condition comes from tunnel vision so narrow as to include only the person and his desires. This calls into question the nature of evil.

Does evil have a reasoned intent to hurt, kill, and destroy or is there an egomaniacal innocence to evil? Could it be that complete evil is actually a blind selfishness? Does evil not arise from a refusal to consider the life, position, or feelings of others? Evil thoughts, actions, and feelings are based on fulfilling one's own desires at the expense or destruction of all others. Feelings and welfare of others do not come into play, nor do they cross the mind of an evil being. The nature of evil is a twisted, childish, innocence; a self-centered and myopic view, where the feelings or life of others is never considered.

How strange and paradoxical; how appropriate that Satan and his demons should take what was so much a part of his own nature and assist man in finding it so abundantly in himself.

As it is written of Satan in the Book of Isaiah:

"How art thou fallen from heaven, O Lucifer, son of the morning! How art thou cut down to the ground, which didst weaken the nations! For thou hast said in thine heart, I will ascend into heaven, I will exalt my throne above the stars of God: I will sit also upon the mount of the congregation, in the sides of the north: I will ascend above the heights of the clouds; I will be like the most High." Isaiah 14:12-14

With evil, the focus is always on oneself. "I want, I will, I can, I feel," and when evil moves in a crowd the words are of little difference. "We will, we shall, we can, we feel..." The nature of evil is simple. It never accounts for others.

As it is written in the records of man, in the ancient book of Jasher:

Jasher 9

And Abram remained in the house of Noah and there knew the Lord and his ways. He served the Lord all the days of his life, and all that generation forgot the Lord, and served other gods of wood and stone, and rebelled all their days.

20 And king Nimrod reigned securely, and all the earth was under his control, and all the earth was of one tongue and words of union.

21 And all the princes of Nimrod and his great men took counsel together: Phut, Mitzraim, Cush and Canaan with their families, and they said to each other, Come let us build ourselves a city and in it a strong tower and its top reaching heaven, and we will make ourselves famed so that we may reign on the whole world, in order that the evil of our enemies may cease from us; that we may reign mightily over them, and that we may not become scattered over the earth on account of their wars.

22 They all went before the king, and they told the king these words, and the king agreed with them in this affair, and he did so.

23 All the families assembled consisting of about six hundred thousand men, and they went to seek an extensive piece of ground to build the city and the tower, and they sought in the whole earth and they found none like one valley at the east of the land of Shinar, about two days' walk, and they journeyed there and they lived there.

24 And they began to make bricks and burn fires to build the city and the tower that they had imagined to complete.

25 And the building of the tower was to them a transgression and a sin, and they began to build it. While they were building against the Lord God of heaven, they imagined in their hearts to war against him and to ascend into heaven.

26 And all these people and all the families divided themselves in three parts; the first said, We will ascend into heaven and fight against him; the second said, We will ascend to heaven and place our own gods there and serve them; and the third part said, We will ascend to heaven and strike him

with bows and spears. And God knew all their works and all their evil thoughts, and he saw the city and the tower which they were building.

27 They built themselves a great city and a very high and strong tower; on account of its height, the mortar and bricks did not reach the builders in their ascent to it until those who went up had completed a full year, and after that, they reached the builders and gave them the mortar and the bricks; thus was it done daily.

28 And behold these ascended and others descended the whole day; and if a brick should fall from their hands and get broken, they would all weep over it; if a man fell and died, none of them would look at him.

29 The Lord knew their thoughts, and it came to pass when they were building they cast the arrows toward the heavens, and all the arrows fell on them filled with blood; when they saw them they said to each other, Certainly we have slain all those that are in heaven.

30 For this was from the Lord in order to cause them to err, and in order to destroy them from off the face of the ground.

31 They built the tower and the city, and they did this thing daily until many days and years were elapsed.

32 And God said to the seventy angels who stood foremost before him, to those who were near to him, saying, Come let us descend and confuse their tongues, that one man shall not understand the language of his neighbor, and they did so to them.

33 From that day following, they forgot each man his neighbor's tongue, and they could not understand to speak in one tongue; when the builder took from the hands of his neighbor lime or stone which he did not order, the builder would cast it away and throw it on his neighbor, that he would die.

34 And they did so many days, and they killed many of them in this manner.

35 The Lord struck the three divisions that were there, and he punished them according to their works and designs; those who said, We will ascend to heaven and serve our gods, became like apes and elephants; those who said, We will strike the heaven with arrows, the Lord killed them, one man through the hand of his neighbor; and the third division of those who said, We will ascend to heaven and fight against him, the Lord scattered them throughout the earth.

36 Those who were left among them, when they knew and understood the evil which was coming on them, turned away from the building, and they also became scattered on the face of the whole earth.

37 And they ceased building the city and the tower; therefore he called that place Babel, for there the Lord confounded the Language of the whole earth; behold it was at the east of the land of Shinar.

38 As to the tower which the sons of men built, the earth opened its mouth and swallowed up one third part thereof, and a fire also descended from heaven and burned another third, and the other third is left to this day; it is of that part which was aloft, and its circumference is three days' walk.

39 Many of the sons of men died in that tower, a people without number.

And so it remains today, that the nature of evil has never changed. Yet, this is only the beginning of the story. Hidden within the most ancient texts are the footprints of evil's origins. Spread through these books are threads of truth left here and there in inherited memories and oral histories dating back to the first recollections of man. In this primal state, evil was born and the story was recorded.

But the records are incomplete. There are loose ends in need of being tied together. Questions remain. Who taught men to build this tower to heaven? Was this the first pyramid?

It is thought that the tower of Babel was a ziggurat, or a step sided pyramid. These were built in ancient Mesopotamia and formed a rectangular stepped tower, sometimes surmounted by a temple. Ziggurats are first attested in the late 3rd millennium B.C. Some think these were the predecessors of the pyramid. The Great Pyramid has encoded in it the radius and diameter of the Earth, as well as the exact length of the solar year and Pi. Out to the fourth decimal place. These measurements were not known on Earth at the time. Did this information come from beyond our world? Were those who taught us angels, demons, or astronauts? For more information on pyramids and the amazing mathematics used in its construction, see appendix "D".

The chronology in the Bible is clear. The building of the tower began soon after the Watchers came to earth. In Genesis 6 the Watchers descended to earth. In Genesis 11 The Tower of Babel was built.

Genesis 11

1 Now the whole world had one language and a common speech. 2 As men moved eastward, they found a plain in Shinar and settled there.
3 They said to each other, "Come, let's make bricks and bake them thoroughly." They used brick instead of stone, and tar for mortar. 4 Then they said, "Come, let us build ourselves a city, with a tower that reaches to the heavens, so that we may make a name for ourselves and not be scattered over the face of the whole earth."
5 But the LORD came down to see the city and the tower that the men were building. 6 The LORD said, "If as one people speaking the same language they have begun to do this, then nothing they plan to do will be impossible for them. 7 Come, let us go down and confuse their language so they will not understand each other."
8 So the LORD scattered them from there over all the earth, and they stopped building the city. 9 That is why it was called Babel, because there the LORD confused the language of the whole world. From there the LORD scattered them over the face of the whole earth.

The science of today was the magic of yesterday. The explanation of men of 200 B.C.E. to 200 A.D. would be formed just as our own explanation would be formed, from the basis of what we know and can relate to. Gods and angels came down from heaven, bred with women, taught mankind secrets of science, and craft.

This begs an age-old question. This brings us to the crux of the matter. Were these angels or visitors? Were they spirits in human form, or human like visitors? Were they from space or are we dealing with an event even more bizarre? Could these angels from heaven be us – from the future – attempting to solve an impending extinction? Had mankind, through some disease or evolution, come to the end of their existence? Were these visitations an attempt to re-seed our genetic line? If so, the experiments went horribly awry.

Enoch
[Chapter 15]

1 And He answered and said to me, and I heard His voice: 'Do not be afraid, Enoch, you righteous man and scribe of righteousness.
2 Approach and hear my voice. Go and say to the Watchers of heaven, for whom you have come to intercede: "You should intercede for men, and not men for you."
3 Why and for what cause have you left the high, holy, and eternal heaven, and had sex with women, and defiled yourselves with the daughters of men and taken to yourselves wives, and done like the children of earth, and begotten giants (as your) sons?
4 Though you were holy, spiritual, living the eternal life, you have defiled yourselves with the blood of women, and have begotten children with the

blood of flesh, and, as the children of men, you have lusted after flesh and blood like those who die and are killed.

5 This is why I have given men wives that they might impregnate them, and have children by them, that deeds might continue on the earth.

6 But you were formerly spiritual, living the eternal life, and immortal for all generations of the world.

7 Therefore I have not appointed wives for you; you are spiritual beings of heaven, and in heaven was your dwelling place.

LUK 20:34 And Jesus answering said unto them, The children of this world marry, and are given in marriage: 35 But they which shall be accounted worthy to obtain that world, and the resurrection from the dead, neither marry, nor are given in marriage: 36 Neither can they die any more: for they are equal unto the angels; and are the children of God, being the children of the resurrection.

8 And now, the giants, who are produced from the spirits and flesh, shall be called evil spirits on the earth,

9 And shall live on the earth. Evil spirits have come out from their bodies because they are born from men and from the holy Watchers, their beginning is of primal origin;

10 They shall be evil spirits on earth, and evil spirits shall they be called spirits of the evil ones. [As for the spirits of heaven, in heaven shall be their dwelling, but as for the spirits of the earth which were born on the earth, on the earth shall be their dwelling.] And the spirits of the giants afflict, oppress, destroy, attack, war, destroy, and cause trouble on the earth.

11 They take no food, but do not hunger or thirst. They cause offences but are not observed.

12 And these spirits shall rise up against the children of men and against the women, because they have proceeded from them in the days of the slaughter and destruction.'

[Chapter 16]

1 'And at the death of the giants, spirits will go out and shall destroy without incurring judgment, coming from their bodies, their flesh shall be destroyed until the day of the consummation, the great judgment in which the age shall be consummated, over the Watchers and the godless, and shall be wholly consummated.'

2 And now as to the Watchers who have sent you (Enoch) to intercede for them, who had been in heaven before,

3 (Say to them): "You were in heaven, but all the mysteries of heaven had not been revealed to you, and you knew worthless ones, and these in the hardness of your hearts you have made known to the women, and through these mysteries women and men work much evil on earth."

4 Say to them therefore: " You have no peace."'

The union of spirit and flesh produced giants, whose spirits were evil and violent. Did the Watchers not foresee the result of their union with the women of earth or was this an experiment in genetics conducted by a superior race?

The sexual deeds of a spiritual beings unleashed the demonic host on earth today. Now there were two hosts of invisible and destructive forces engaged in the torment and destruction of mankind. Satan and his host seek to enslave the souls of men. Evil spirits of the giants proceed out with hateful intent.

Jubilees

20 In the twenty-eighth jubilee Noah began to direct his sons in the ordinances and commandments, and all the judgments that he knew, and he exhorted his sons to observe righteousness, and to cover the shame of their flesh, and to bless their Creator, and honor father and mother, and love their neighbor, and guard their souls from fornication and uncleanness and all iniquity.

21 Because of these three things came the flood on the earth, namely, the fornication that the Watchers committed against the law of their ordinances when they went whoring after the daughters of men, and took themselves wives of all they chose, and they made the beginning of uncleanness.

22 And they begat sons, the naphilim (Naphidim), and they were all dissimilar, and they devoured one another, and the Giants killed the Naphil, and the Naphil killed the Eljo, and the Eljo killed mankind, and one man killed one another.

23 Every one committed himself to crime and injustice and to shed much blood, and the earth was filled with sin.

24 After this they sinned against the beasts and birds, and all that moved and walked on the earth, and much blood was shed on the earth, and men continually desired only what was useless and evil.

25 And the Lord destroyed everything from the face of the earth. Because of the wickedness of their deeds, and because of the blood they had shed over all the earth, He destroyed everything. "

26 We were left, I and you, my sons, and everything that entered with us into the ark, and behold I see your works before me that you do not walk in righteousness, for in the path of destruction you have begun to walk, and you are turning one against another, and are envious one of another, and so it comes that you are not in harmony, my sons, each with his brother.

27 For I see the demons have begun their seductions against you and against your children and now I fear on your behalf, that after my death you will shed the blood of men on the earth, and that you, too, will be destroyed from the face of the earth.

28 For whoever sheds man's blood, and who ever eats the blood of any flesh, shall all be destroyed from the earth.

29 There shall be no man left that eats blood, or that sheds the blood of man on the earth, nor shall there be left to him any offspring or descendants living under heaven. Into the abode of the dead shall they go, and into the place of condemnation shall they descend, and into the darkness of the deep shall they all be removed by a violent death.

The union of spirit and flesh (or visitor and woman) produced three distinct races, the giants, the nethilim, and the eljo. Was this because the union of flesh and spirit was unstable and genetically mutable, or are we only assuming the Watchers were a single class of angelic beings? What if "Watcher" was the title of a post or assignment, and not a class of being?

The Bible speaks of three classes of heavenly beings. There are cherubim, seraphim, and angels. If a number of these three classes of beings were assigned to the post of watcher the mystery of the divergent species and the three types of offspring would be solved. Angels, seraphim, and cherubim took on human form and took up habitation on earth. They were spiritual beings processing power and knowledge. Each type of spiritual entity produced a different offspring. The some of angelic children became the men of renown. These were Hercules, Achilles and men of legend.

There were those whom we are told killed mankind and became the monsters of our nightmare, the Cyclops, and those beings that raged against men.

The others became the spiritual creatures of myth. These were the invisible creatures that tormented man with their demonic powers. When they were destroyed because of their lawlessness and violence the spirits inhabiting their cages of flesh and blood escaped to continue their bloodlust unseen and unstoppable.

The depth of sin and perversion was vast and God cleansed the earth of sin, leaving only eight people to replenish the earth. Because of the Watchers, the flood came.

Lost Book of Enoch

Chapter 9

6 Look at what Azazel has done, who hath taught all unrighteousness on earth and revealed the eternal secrets which were made and kept in heaven, which men were striving to learn:

7 And Semjaza, who taught spells, to whom you gave authority to rule over his associates.

8 And they have gone to the daughters of men on the earth, and have had sex with the women, and have defiled themselves, and revealed to them all kinds of sins.

GEN 6:4 There were giants in the earth in those days; and also after that, when the sons of God came in unto the daughters of men, and they bare children to them, the same became mighty men which were of old, men of renown.

9 And the women have borne giants, and the whole earth has thereby been filled with blood and unrighteousness.

GEN 6:5 And GOD saw that the wickedness of man was great in the earth, and that every imagination of the thoughts of his heart was only evil continually. 6 And it repented the LORD that he had made man on the earth, and it grieved him at his heart.

10 And now, behold, the souls of those who have died are crying out and making their petition to the gates of heaven, and their lament has ascended and cannot cease because of the lawless deeds which are done on the earth.

11 And you know all things before they come to pass, and you see these things and you have permitted them, and say nothing to us about these things. What are we to do with them about these things?'

[Chapter 10]

1 Then said the Most High, the Great and Holy One, Uriel go to the son of Lamech.

2 Say to him: 'Go to Noah and tell him in my name "Hide yourself!" and reveal to him the end that is approaching: that the whole earth will be destroyed, and a flood is about to come on the whole earth, and will destroy everything on it.'

GEN 7:4 For yet seven days, and I will cause it to rain upon the earth forty days and forty nights; and every living substance that I have made will I destroy from off the face of the earth.

3 'And now instruct him as to what he must do to escape that his offspring may be preserved for all the generations of the world.'

Book of Enoch

13 And I, Enoch, answered and said to him: 'The Lord will do a new thing on the earth, and this I have already seen in a vision, and make known to you that in the generation of my father Jared some of the angels of heaven violated the word of the Lord. And they commited sin and broke the law,

and have had sex (united themselves) with women and committed sin with them, and have married some of them, and have had children by them.

14 And they shall produce on the earth giants not according to the spirit, but according to the flesh, and there shall be a great punishment on the earth, and the earth shall be cleansed from all impurity.

15 There shall come a great destruction over the whole earth, and there shall be a flood (deluge) and a great destruction for one year.

16 And this son who has been born to you shall be left on the earth, and his three children shall be saved with him: when all mankind that are on the earth shall die, he and his sons shall be saved.

Book Of Jubilees

19 And what was and what will be he (Enoch) saw in a vision of his sleep, as it will happen to the children of men throughout their generations until the day of judgment; he saw and understood everything, and wrote his testimony, and placed the testimony on earth for all the children of men and for their generations.

20 In the twelfth jubilee, in the seventh week of it, he took to himself a wife, and her name was Edna, the daughter of Danel, the daughter of his father's brother, and in the sixth year in this week she gave birth to a son and he called his name Methuselah.

21 He was with the angels of God these six jubilees of years, and they showed him everything that is on earth and in the heavens, the rule of the sun, and he wrote down everything.

22 And he testified to the Watchers, who had sinned with the daughters of men; for these had begun to unite themselves, so as to be defiled with the daughters of men, and Enoch testified against them all.

23 And he was taken from among the children of men, and we conducted him into the Garden of Eden in majesty and honor, and there he wrote

down the condemnation and judgment of the world, and all the wickedness of the children of men.

24 Because of it God brought the waters of the flood on all the land of Eden; for there he was set as a sign and that he should testify against all the children of men, that he should recount all the deeds of the generations until the day of condemnation.

Come as it may, no flood, nor any death could kill the evil spirits. God only deprived them of willing hosts, that is, until Noah and his family began to multiply. In an family, holy or not, there will always be evil, waiting to come forth.

Book of Jubilees

27 For I see the demons have begun their seductions against you and against your children and now I fear on your behalf, that after my death you will shed the blood of men on the earth, and that you, too, will be destroyed from the face of the earth.

28 For whoever sheds man's blood, and who ever eats the blood of any flesh, shall all be destroyed from the earth.

29 There shall be no man left that eats blood, or that sheds the blood of man on the earth, nor shall there be left to him any offspring or descendants living under heaven. Into the abode of the dead shall they go, and into the place of condemnation shall they descend, and into the darkness of the deep shall they all be removed by a violent death.

30 Do not smear blood on yourself or let it remain on you. Out of all the blood that shall be shed and out of all the days in which you have killed any beasts or cattle or whatever flies on the earth you must do a good work to your souls by covering that which has been shed on the face of the earth.

31 You shall not be like him who eats blood, but guard yourselves that none may eat blood before you, cover the blood, for thus have I been commanded to testify to you and your children, together with all flesh.

32 Do not permit the soul (life) to be eaten with the flesh, that your blood, which is your life, may not be required at the hand of any flesh that sheds it on the earth.

33 For the earth will not be clean from the blood that has been shed on it, for only through the blood of him that shed it will the earth be purified throughout all its generations.

Could it be that Satan and his hosts are not responsible for demonic possessions? Might it be that they are responsible only for the testing and trails of mankind? Is it the unbridled spirits of the unholy union of Watcher and woman that torments, oppresses, and enslaves us?

Book of Jubilees
Chapter 10]

1 In the third week of this jubilee the unclean demons began to lead astray the children of the sons of Noah, and to make them sin and to destroy them.

2 The sons of Noah came to Noah their father, and they told him about the demons that were leading astray and blinding and slaying his sons' sons.

3 And he prayed before the Lord his God, and said, "God of the spirits of all flesh, who have shown mercy to me and have spared me and my sons from the waters of the flood, and have not caused me to die as You did the sons of perdition; For Your grace has been great toward me, and great has been Your mercy to my soul. Let Your grace be lifted up on my sons, and do not let the wicked spirits rule over them or they will destroy them from the earth.

4 But bless me and my sons, so that we may increase and multiply and replenish the earth.

5 You know how Your Watchers, the fathers of these spirits, acted in my day, and as for these spirits which are living, imprison them and hold them fast in the place of condemnation, and let them not bring destruction on the sons of your servant, my God; for these are like cancer and are created in order to destroy.

6 Let them not rule over the spirits of the living; for You alone can exercise dominion over them. And let them not have power over the sons of the righteous from now and forever."

7 And the Lord our God commanded us (angels) to bind all of them.

8 The chief of the spirits, Mastema (Satan), came and said, "Lord, Creator, let some of them remain before me, and let them listen to my voice, and do all that I shall say to them; for if some of them are not left to me, I shall not be able to execute the power of my will on the sons of men, for these are for corruption and leading astray before my judgment, for great is the wickedness of the sons of men."

9 He said, "Let one-tenth of them remain before him, and let nine-tenths of them descend into the place of condemnation."

10 He commanded one of us to teach Noah all their medicines, for He knew that they would not walk in uprightness, nor strive in righteousness.

MAT 8:28- 32 And when he was come to the other side into the country of the Gergesenes, there met him two possessed with devils, coming out of the tombs, exceeding fierce, so that no man might pass by that way.

29And, behold, they cried out, saying, What have we to do with thee, Jesus, thou Son of God? art thou come hither to torment us before the time?

30And there was a good way off from them an herd of many swine feeding.

31So the devils besought him, saying, If thou cast us out, suffer us to go away into the herd of swine.

32And he said unto them, Go. And when they were come out, they went into the herd of swine: and, behold, the whole herd of swine ran violently down a steep place into the sea, and perished in the waters.

Why did the demons ask to go into the swine? They were accustomed to inhabiting animals as well as humans. This is the reason God commanded Saul, king of Israel, to kill all people and animals of their enemies. It was important enough that when Saul disobeyed, God chose not to continue his bloodline as king.

1 Samuel 15

1Samuel also said unto Saul, The LORD sent me to anoint thee to be king over his people, over Israel: now therefore hearken thou unto the voice of the words of the LORD.

2Thus saith the LORD of hosts, I remember that which Amalek did to Israel, how he laid wait for him in the way, when he came up from Egypt.

3Now go and smite Amalek, and utterly destroy all that they have, and spare them not; but slay both man and woman, infant and suckling, ox and sheep, camel and ass.

4And Saul gathered the people together, and numbered them in Telaim, two hundred thousand footmen, and ten thousand men of Judah.

5And Saul came to a city of Amalek, and laid wait in the valley.

6And Saul said unto the Kenites, Go, depart, get you down from among the Amalekites, lest I destroy you with them: for ye shewed kindness to all the children of Israel, when they came up out of Egypt. So the Kenites departed from among the Amalekites.

7And Saul smote the Amalekites from Havilah until thou comest to Shur, that is over against Egypt.

8And he took Agag the king of the Amalekites alive, and utterly destroyed all the people with the edge of the sword.

9But Saul and the people spared Agag, and the best of the sheep, and of the oxen, and of the fatlings, and the lambs, and all that was good, and would not utterly destroy them: but every thing that was vile and refuse, that they destroyed utterly.

10Then came the word of the LORD unto Samuel, saying,

11It repenteth me that I have set up Saul to be king: for he is turned back from following me, and hath not performed my commandments. And it grieved Samuel; and he cried unto the LORD all night.

12And when Samuel rose early to meet Saul in the morning, it was told Samuel, saying, Saul came to Carmel, and, behold, he set him up a place, and is gone about, and passed on, and gone down to Gilgal.

13And Samuel came to Saul: and Saul said unto him, Blessed be thou of the LORD: I have performed the commandment of the LORD.

14And Samuel said, What meaneth then this bleating of the sheep in mine ears, and the lowing of the oxen which I hear?

15And Saul said, They have brought them from the Amalekites: for the people spared the best of the sheep and of the oxen, to sacrifice unto the LORD thy God; and the rest we have utterly destroyed.

16Then Samuel said unto Saul, Stay, and I will tell thee what the LORD hath said to me this night. And he said unto him, Say on.

17And Samuel said, When thou wast little in thine own sight, wast thou not made the head of the tribes of Israel, and the LORD anointed thee king over Israel?

18And the LORD sent thee on a journey, and said, Go and utterly destroy the sinners, the Amalekites, and fight against them until they be consumed.

19Wherefore then didst thou not obey the voice of the LORD, but didst fly upon the spoil, and didst evil in the sight of the LORD?

20And Saul said unto Samuel, Yea, I have obeyed the voice of the LORD, and have gone the way which the LORD sent me, and have brought Agag the king of Amalek, and have utterly destroyed the Amalekites.

21But the people took of the spoil, sheep and oxen, the chief of the things which should have been utterly destroyed, to sacrifice unto the LORD thy God in Gilgal.

22And Samuel said, Hath the LORD as great delight in burnt offerings and sacrifices, as in obeying the voice of the LORD? Behold, to obey is better than sacrifice, and to hearken than the fat of rams.

23For rebellion is as the sin of witchcraft, and stubbornness is as iniquity and idolatry. Because thou hast rejected the word of the LORD, he hath also rejected thee from being king.

24And Saul said unto Samuel, I have sinned: for I have transgressed the commandment of the LORD, and thy words: because I feared the people, and obeyed their voice.

25Now therefore, I pray thee, pardon my sin, and turn again with me, that I may worship the LORD.

26And Samuel said unto Saul, I will not return with thee: for thou hast rejected the word of the LORD, and the LORD hath rejected thee from being king over Israel.

27And as Samuel turned about to go away, he laid hold upon the skirt of his mantle, and it rent.

28And Samuel said unto him, The LORD hath rent the kingdom of Israel from thee this day, and hath given it to a neighbour of thine, that is better than thou.

29And also the Strength of Israel will not lie nor repent: for he is not a man, that he should repent.

30Then he said, I have sinned: yet honour me now, I pray thee, before the elders of my people, and before Israel, and turn again with me, that I may worship the LORD thy God.

31So Samuel turned again after Saul; and Saul worshipped the LORD.

32Then said Samuel, Bring ye hither to me Agag the king of the Amalekites. And Agag came unto him delicately. And Agag said, Surely the bitterness of death is past.

33And Samuel said, As thy sword hath made women childless, so shall thy mother be childless among women. And Samuel hewed Agag in pieces before the LORD in Gilgal.

34Then Samuel went to Ramah; and Saul went up to his house to Gibeah of Saul.

35And Samuel came no more to see Saul until the day of his death: nevertheless Samuel mourned for Saul: and the LORD repented that he had made Saul king over Israel.

Panoramic View

What you are about to read is not in any Bible. It is a story drawn from the pages of some of the oldest writings on earth. The stories told in these ancient pages were both historical and prophetic. All of them spoke of the same occurrences, those of the birth, history, and destruction of evil.

From the books of Jasher, Jubilees, Enoch, the War Scrolls, the Bible, and others, each narrator tells a version of the same events, rich in detail. By combining all the narratives and removing repetitive events we come to a place of awe, where the specific aspects before us are amazing and finely painted.

The reader is never told what line, word, or phrase came from any particular book. The story is written, as any story should be, without pause. Only the myth of Lilith is set apart by being printed in italicized font. This was done to distinguish a traditional oral myth of the Middle Ages from those books honored in the halls of much greater antiquity.

(All of these books can be found in one volume called, "The Lost Books of the Bible: The Great Rejected Texts," by Joseph Lumpkin, published by Fifth Estate.)

The history of angels and demons begs the deepest and most profound questions. Was evil created, or discovered within us as a consequence of free will? Did God, who created everything, create evil? Did He who is omniscient realize what would happen when He gave all sentient beings the ability to choose? How did it begin, and where will it end?

The Story of Evil

In the beginning, God created the heavens and the earth, and the earth was formless, vacant, and chaotic. Darkness was everywhere and no light was seen except God, Himself. God formed the earth, divided the lands and waters, and set the clouds, sky, and earth in place. He made the sun and moon and all the planets and set their courses, dividing day from night. All heavenly bodies were assigned their times and paths and none varied from God's word.

God created all things living, and then he created man. He created a man and a woman and gave them dominion over all things. God named the man Adam, and the woman He named Lilith. Both were formed from the dust of the earth and in both God breathed the breath of life. They became human souls and God endowed them with the power of speech.

Created at the same time, in the same way, there was no master, no leader, and only bickering between them. Lilith said, "I will not be below you, in life or during sex. I want the superior position". But Adam would not relent and insisted God had created him to be the head of the family and in the affairs of earth. Lilith was enraged and would not submit.

Then God communed with Adam in the cool of the evening and as he entered into His presence, Adam appealed to God. As God fellowshipped with them, they reasoned together, Adam, Lilith, and the living God. But Lilith would not listen to God or Adam. Seeing that with two people of equal authority there could be no solution, Lilith became frustrated, angry, and intractable. Finally, enraged and defiant, she pronounced the holy and ineffable name of God. Corrupting the power of the name, she flew into the air, changing form, and disappeared, soaring out of sight.

Adam stood alone, confused, praying. "Lord of the universe," he said, "The woman you gave me has run away." At once, three holy angels were dispatched to bring her back to Adam. The angels overtook Lilith as she passed over the sea, in the area where Moses would later pass through. The angels ordered Lilith to come with them in the name and by the authority of the most high God, but she refused. As her rebellion increased, she changed, becoming more and more ugly and demonic.

God spoke into Lilith's heart, saying, "You have chosen this evil path, and so shall you become evil. You are cursed from now until the end of days." Lilith spoke to the angels and said, "I have become this, created to cause sickness, to kill children, which I will never have, and to torment men." With these words, she completed her demonic transformation. Her form was that of a succubus.

Confined to the night, she was destined to roam the earth, seeking newborn babes, stealing their lives, and strangling them in their sleep. She torments men even now, causing lust and evil dreams. Her rebellious and evil spirit forever traps her. Bound in the darkness of her own heart, Lilith became the mistress and lover to legions of demons. And Adam's countenance fell and he mourned for he had loved Lilith, and he was again alone and lonely.

God said, "It is not good for man to be alone." And the Lord God caused a deep sleep to fall on him, and he slept, and He took from Adam a rib from among his ribs for the woman, and this rib was the origin of the woman. And He built up the flesh in its place, and created the woman. He awakened Adam out of his sleep. On awakening Adam rose on the sixth day, and God brought her to Adam, and he knew her, and said to her, "This is now bone of my bones and flesh of my flesh; she shall be called woman for she was taken from man, and she shall be called my wife; because she was taken from her husband."

Her name will be Eve, for she will be the mother of all. Therefore shall man and wife become one. Because of this a man shall leave his father and his mother, and cling to his wife, and they shall be one flesh.

In the first week of creation Adam was created, and from his rib, his wife was formed. In the second week God showed her to him. For this reason the commandment was given to keep in the times of their defilement (from birth). A male should be purified in seven days and for a female twice seven days. After Adam had completed forty days in the land where he had been created, the angels brought him into the garden of Eden to till and keep it, but his wife the angels brought in on the eightieth day, and after this she entered into the garden of Eden.

In these days there was a great war in heaven. Lucifer, who is known as the son of the morning, amassed one third of the angels of heaven and fought for supremacy. In righteous anger, God arose and spoke to Lucifer, "Hell from beneath is moved for thee to meet thee at thy coming; it stirreth up the dead for thee, even all the chief ones of the earth; it hath raised up from their thrones all the kings of the nations.

"All shall speak and say unto thee, Art thou also become weak as we? Art thou become like unto us? Thy pomp is brought you down to the grave, and the noise of thy viols. The worm is spread under thee, and the worms cover thee. How art thou fallen from heaven, O Lucifer, son of the morning! How art thou cut down to the ground, you who didst weaken the nations! For thou hast said in thine heart, I will ascend into heaven, I will exalt my throne above the stars of God: I will sit also upon the mount of the congregation, in the sides of the north.

"I will ascend above the heights of the clouds; I will be like the most High. Yet thou shalt be brought down to hell, to the sides of the pit."

But Lucifer did not heed the words of God, and the war in heaven began.

Michael and his host fought against Lucifer and his army and Michael prevailed. And Lucifer, whose name became Satan, the devil, and Mastema, was thrown down to the earth in defeat and dishonor. And Jesus, who is the word of God and with him from the beginning, watched as Lucifer was defeated in heaven and cast down. And he said unto them, "I beheld Satan as lightning fall from heaven." Thus, the war in heaven would be waged on earth for the prize of the souls of men.

Then Satan entered into the serpent, for the serpent was willing. And he waited until the time of deceit was at hand.

After the completion of exactly seven years there, and in the second month, on the seventeenth day of the month, the serpent, which God had created with them in the earth, came to Eve to incite them to go contrary to the command of God which he had given them. The serpent approached the woman, and the serpent said to the woman, "Has God commanded you saying, you shall not eat of every tree of the garden?"

She said to it, "God said to us, 'Of all the fruit of the trees of the garden, eat; but of the fruit of the tree which is in the middle of the garden,' God said to us, 'You shall not eat of it, neither shall you touch it, or you shall die.'"

The serpent said to the woman, "You shall not surely die. God knows if you were to eat the fruit of the tree your eyes would be opened and you would become as a god." And the woman saw the tree that it was beautiful and pleasant to the eye, and that its fruit was good for food. And the serpent enticed and persuaded the woman to eat from the tree of knowledge, and the woman listened to the voice of the serpent, and she went contrary to the word of God, and took from the tree of the knowledge of good and evil. And she took of it and ate. And she took from it and gave also to her husband and he ate. For, the serpent said, "You will not surely die. God knows that on the day you shall eat of it, your eyes will be opened, and you will be as gods, and you will know good and evil."

And Adam and his wife went contrary to the command of God which he commanded them, and God knew it, and his anger was set ablaze against them and he cursed them.

And the Lord God drove them that day from the Garden of Eden, to till the ground from which they were taken, and they went and lived at the east of the garden of Eden.

First, Eve covered her shame with fig leaves and then she gave the fruit to Adam and he ate, and his eyes were opened, and he saw that he was naked.

He took fig leaves and sewed them together, and made an apron for himself, and covered his shame.

God cursed the serpent, and was very angry at it forever. And He was very angry with the woman, because she listened to the voice of the serpent, and ate; and He said to her, "I will vastly multiply your sorrow and your pains, in sorrow you will bring forth children, and your master shall be your husband, and he will rule over you."

To Adam also he said, " Because you have listened to the voice of your wife, and have eaten of the tree of which I commanded you not to eat, cursed be the ground for your sake, thorns and thistles shall it produce for you, and you will eat your bread in the sweat of your face, until you return to the earth from where you were taken; for earth you are, and to earth will you return."

And God made for them coats of skin, and clothed them, and sent them out from the Garden of Eden.

God said to Adam, "I have ordained days and years on this earth, and you and your descendants shall live and walk in them until the days and years are fulfilled. Then I shall send the Word that created you and against which you have transgressed the Word that made you come out of the garden and that raised you when you were fallen. Yes, this is the Word that will again save you when the five and a half days are fulfilled."

But when Adam heard these words from God, and of the great five and a half days he did not understand the meaning of them. For Adam was thinking there would be only five and a half days for him until the end of the world. And Adam cried and prayed to God to explain it to him. Then God in his mercy for Adam who was made after His own image and likeness explained to him that these were 5,000 and 500 years and how (the) One would then come and save him and his descendants. But before that, God had made this covenant with our father, Adam, in the same terms before he came out of the garden, when he was by the tree where Eve took of the fruit and gave it to him to eat. Because, when our father, Adam, came out of the garden he passed by that tree and saw how God had changed the appearance of it into another form and how it had shriveled.

And as Adam went to it he feared, trembled, and fell down. But God in His mercy lifted him up and then made this covenant with him. Also, when Adam was by the gate of the garden he saw the cherub with a sword of flashing fire in his hand, and the cherub grew angry and frowned at him. Both Adam and Eve became afraid of the cherub and thought he meant to put them to death. So they fell on their faces, trembling with fear. But he had pity on them and showed them mercy. And turning from them, he went up to heaven and prayed to the Lord, and said; "Lord, You sent me to watch at the gate of the garden, with a sword of fire. But when Your servants, Adam and Eve, saw me, they fell on their faces, and were as dead. O my Lord, what shall we do to Your servants?"

Then God had pity on them, and showed them mercy, and sent

His Angel to keep the garden. And the Word of the Lord came to Adam and Eve, and raised them up. And the Lord said to Adam, "I told you that at the end of the five and a half days I will send my Word and save you. Therefore, strengthen your heart and stay in the Cave of Treasures, of which I have spoken to you before." And when Adam heard this Word from God he was comforted with that which God had told him. For He had told him how He would save him.

But God had said to him, of your own free will have you transgressed through your desire for divinity, greatness, and an exalted state, such as I have; therefore I deprived you of the bright nature which you had then, and I made you come out of the garden to this land, rough and full of trouble. If only you had not transgressed My commandment and had kept My law, and had not eaten of the fruit of the tree which I told you not to come near! And there were fruit trees in the garden better than that one.

But the wicked Satan did not keep his faith and had no good intent towards Me, and although I had created him he considered Me to be useless, and he sought the Godhead for himself. For this I hurled him down from heaven so that he could not remain in his first estate. It was he who made the tree appear pleasant to your eyes until you ate of it by believing his words. Thus have you transgressed My commandment, and therefore I have brought on you all these sorrows. For I am God the Creator, who, when I created My creatures, did not intend to destroy them. But after they had greatly roused My anger I punished them with grievous plagues until they repented. But, if on the contrary they still continue hardened in their transgression they shall be under a curse forever." But Adam and Even continued to seek God and pray with fervent hearts.

Satan, the hater of all that is good, saw how they continued in prayer, and how God communed with them, and comforted them, and how He had accepted their offering. Then Satan made a phantasm. He began by transforming his hosts. In his hands was a shining, glimmering fire, and they were in a huge light. Then, he placed his throne near the mouth of the cave, because he could not enter it due to their prayers. And he shown light into the cave until the cave glistened over Adam and Eve while his hosts began to sing praises. Satan did this so that when Adam saw the light he would think to himself that it was a heavenly light and that Satan's hosts were angels and that God had sent them to watch at the cave, and give him light in the darkness.

Satan planned that when Adam came out of the cave and saw them and Adam and Eve bowed to Satan, then he would overcome Adam and humble him before God a second time. When, therefore, Adam and Eve saw the light, thinking it was real, they strengthened their hearts. Then, as they were trembling, Adam said to Eve: "Look at that great light, and at those many songs of praise, and at that host standing outside who won't come into our cave. Why don't they tell us what they want or where they are from or what the meaning of this light is or what those praises are or why they have been sent to this place, and why they won't come in? If they were from God, they would come into the cave with us and would tell us why they were sent."

Then Adam stood up and prayed to God with a burning heart and said: "O Lord, is there in the world another god besides You who created angels and filled them with light, and sent them to keep us, who would come with them? But, look, we see these hosts that stand at the mouth of the cave. They are in a great light and they sing loud praises. If they are of some other god(s) than You, tell me, and if they are sent by you, inform me of the reason for which You have sent them." No sooner had Adam said this, than an angel from God appeared to him in the cave, who said to him, "O Adam, fear not. This is Satan and his hosts. He wishes to deceive you as he deceived you at first. For the first time, he was hidden in the serpent, but this time he is come to you in the likeness of an angel of light in order that, when you worshipped him, he might enslave you in the very presence of God."

Then the angel went from Adam and seized Satan at the opening of the cave, and stripped him of the false image (lie / pretense) he had assumed and brought him in his own hideous form to Adam and Eve who were afraid of him when they saw him.

But Satan, the hater of all that is good, thought to himself: "God has promised salvation to Adam by covenant, and promised that He would deliver him from all the hardships that have befallen him, but God has not promised me by covenant, and will not deliver me out of my hardships. He has promised Adam that He should make him and his descendants live in the kingdom that I once lived in. I will kill Adam. The earth shall be rid of him. The earth shall be left to me alone. When he is dead he will not have any descendants left to inherit the kingdom and it will remain my own realm. God will then be wanting me, and He will restore it to me and my hosts." And so Satan never stopped seeking to destroy Adam and Eve.

After this Satan, the hater of all that is good, took the form of an angel, and two others with him. So, they looked like the three angels who had brought to Adam gold, incense, and myrrh. They came to Adam and Eve while they were under the tree, and greeted Adam and Eve with friendly words that were full of deceit. But when Adam and Eve saw their friendly countenance and heard their sweet speech, Adam rose, welcomed them, and brought them to Eve and they remained all together. Adam's heart was happy all the while because he thought that they were the same angels, who had brought him gold, incense, and myrrh. This was because when they came to Adam the first time peace and joy came over him from them because they brought him good gifts.

So Adam thought that they had come a second time to give him other gifts to make him rejoice. He did not know it was Satan, therefore he received them with joy and associated with them. Then Satan, the tallest of them, said, "Rejoice, Adam, and be glad. Look, God has sent us to you to tell you something." And Adam said, "What is it?" Then Satan said, "It is a simple thing, but it is the Word of God. Will you accept it from us and do it? If you will not accept it, we will return to God and tell Him that you would not receive His Word." And Satan continued, saying to Adam, "Don't be afraid and don't shake. Don't you know us?" But Adam said, "I do not know you." Then Satan said to him, "I am the angel that brought you gold and took it to the cave. This other angel is the one that brought you incense. And that third angel is the one who brought you myrrh when you were on top of the mountain. It was he who carried you to the cave. It was our other fellow angels who lifted you to the cave. God has not sent them with us this time because He said to us, 'You will be enough'. "

So when Adam heard these words he believed them, and said to the angels, "Speak the Word of God, and I will receive it." And Satan said to him, "Swear and promise me that you will receive it." Then Adam said, "I do not know how to swear and promise." And Satan said to him, "Hold out your hand and put it inside my hand."

Then Adam held out his hand, and put it into Satan's hand. Satan said to him, "Now say this; As God who raised the stars in heaven, and established the dry ground on the waters, and has created me out of the four elements, and out of the dust of the earth, and is logical and true does speak, I will not break my promise, nor abandon my word." And Adam swore.

Then Satan said to him, "Look, some time has passed since you came out of the garden, and you do not know wickedness or evil. But now God says to you, to take Eve who came out of your side, and marry her so that she will bear you children to comfort you and to drive from you trouble and sorrow. This thing is not difficult and there is nothing morally wrong in it for you. But when Adam heard these words from Satan, he sorrowed much, because of his oath and his promise. And he said, "Shall I commit adultery with my flesh and my bones, and shall I sin against myself, so that God will destroy me and blot me out from the face of the earth?

But from that day Adam struggled in his mind about marrying Eve, because he was afraid that if he did it, God would be angry with him. Then Adam and Eve went to the river of water, and sat on the bank, as people do when they enjoy themselves. But Satan was jealous of them and planned to destroy them.

Therefore Satan worked this apparition before Adam and Eve, because he sought to kill him, and to make him disappear from off the face of the earth. Meanwhile the fire of immorality came over Adam and he thought of committing transgression. But he restrained himself, fearing that if he followed the advice of Satan, God would put him to death. Then Adam and Eve got up and prayed to God, while Satan and his hosts went down into the river in front of Adam and Eve so they would see them going back to their own world.

Then Adam and Eve went back to the Cave of Treasures, as they usually did around evening time. And they both got up and prayed to God that night. Adam remained standing in prayer but did not know how to pray because of the thoughts in his heart about marrying Eve. And he continued this way until morning. When light came up, Adam said to Eve, "Get up, let us go below the mountain where they brought us gold and let us ask the Lord concerning this matter." Then Eve said, "What is that matter, Adam?" And he answered her, "That I may request the Lord to inform me about marrying you because I will not do it without His permission or else He will kill you and me. For those devils have set my heart on fire with thoughts of what they showed us in their sinful visions. Then Eve said to Adam, "Why do we need to go to the foot of the mountain? Let us rather stand up and pray in our cave to God to let us know whether this advice is good or not."

Then Adam rose up in prayer and said, "O God, you know that we transgressed against you, and from the moment we sinned we were stripped of our bright nature, and our body became brutish, requiring food and drink, and with animal desires. Command us, O God, not to give way to them without Your permission, for fear that You will turn us into nothing. If you do not give us permission we will be overcome and follow that advice of Satan, and You will again kill us. If not, then take our souls from us and let us be rid of this animal lust. And if You give us no order about this thing then separate Eve from me and me from her, and place us each far away from the other.

Then, O God, if You separate us from each other the devils will deceive us with their apparitions that resemble us, and destroy our hearts, and defile our thoughts towards each other. If our heart is not toward each other it will be toward them, through their appearance when the devils come to us in our likeness." Here Adam ended his prayer.

Then God considered the words of Adam that they were true, and that he could not wait long for His order, respecting the counsel of Satan. And God approved Adam in what he had thought concerning this, and in the prayer he had offered in His presence; and the Word of God came to Adam.

After that, God sent His angel who had brought gold, and the angel who had brought incense, and the angel who had brought myrrh to Adam, that they should inform him respecting his marriage to Eve. Then those angels said to Adam, "Take the gold and give it to Eve as a wedding gift, and promise to marry her; then give her some incense and myrrh as a present; and you both will be one flesh." Adam obeyed the angels, and took the gold and put it into Eve's bosom in her garment; and promised to marry her with his hand. Then the angels commanded Adam and Eve to get up and pray forty days and forty nights; when that was done, then Adam was to have sexual intercourse with his wife; for then this would be an act pure and undefiled; so that he would have children who would multiply, and replenish the face of the earth. And God spoke to Adam and Eve and said, "Be fruitful, multiply, and replenish the earth."

Adam knew his wife Eve and she bore two sons and three daughters. In the third week in the second jubilee she gave birth to Cain, and in the fourth jubilee she gave birth to Abel, and in the fifth jubilee she gave birth to her daughter Awan.

In the first year of the third jubilee, Cain talked with Abel his brother. It was at the expiration of a few years, that they had brought a first-fruit offering to the Lord, and Cain brought from the fruit of the ground, and Abel brought from the firstlings of his flock from the fat thereof, and God turned and inclined to Abel and his offering, and a fire came down from the Lord from heaven and consumed it. And to Cain and his offering the Lord did not turn, and he did not incline to it, for he had brought from the inferior fruit of the ground before the Lord, and Cain was jealous against his brother Abel on account of this, and he sought an opportunity to kill him.

And Cain was even more jealous of his brother because Abel was promised to marry Cain's sister and Cain was to marry Abel's sister but the sister promised to Abel was more beautiful. Cain lusted for his own sister and wished to marry her.

And in some time after, Cain and Abel his brother, went one day into the field to do their work; and they were both in the field, Cain farming and plowing his ground, and Abel feeding his flock; and the flock passed through that part which Cain had plowed in the ground, and it sorely grieved Cain on this account. And Cain approached his brother Abel in anger, and he said to him, "What gives you the right to come and live here and bring your flock to feed in my land?" And Abel answered his brother Cain and said to him, "What gives you the right to eat the flesh of my flock and clothe yourself with their wool? Take off the wool of my sheep with which you have clothed yourself, and pay me for their resources you have used and flesh which you have eaten, and when you shall have done this, I will then go from your land as you have said."

And Cain said to his brother Abel, "Certainly if I kill you this day, who will require your blood from me?" And Abel answered Cain, saying, "Certainly God who has made us in the earth, he will avenge my cause, and he will require my blood from you should you kill me, for the Lord is the judge and arbiter, and it is he who will repay man according to his evil, and the wicked man according to the wickedness that he may do upon earth. And now, if you should kill me here, certainly God knows your secret views, and will judge you for the evil which you declared to do to me this day."

And when Cain heard the words which Abel his brother had spoken, the anger of Cain was set ablaze against his brother Abel for declaring this thing. And Cain hurried and rose up, and took the iron part of his plowing instrument, with which he suddenly struck his brother and he killed him, and Cain spilled the blood of his brother Abel upon the earth, and the blood of Abel streamed upon the earth before the flock.

And after this Cain repented of having slain his brother, and he was sadly grieved, and he wept over him and it troubled him exceedingly. And Cain rose up and dug a hole in the field, wherein he put his brother's body, and he turned the dust over it.

And the Lord said unto Cain, "Where is Abel thy brother?" And he said, "I know not: Am I my brother's keeper?" And he said, "What hast thou done? The voice of thy brother's blood crieth unto me from the ground. And now art thou cursed from the earth, which hath opened her mouth to receive thy brother's blood from thy hand; When thou tillest the ground, it shall not henceforth yield unto thee her strength; a fugitive and a vagabond shalt thou be in the earth."

"For you have slain your brother and have lied before me, and imagined in your heart that I saw you not, nor knew all your actions. But you did this thing and did kill your brother for naught, for he spoke rightly to you, and now therefore, cursed be you from the ground which opened its mouth to receive your brother's blood from your hand, and wherein you did bury him."

"And it shall be when you shall till it, it shall no more give you its strength as in the beginning, for thorns and thistles shall the ground produce, and you shall be moving and wandering in the earth until the day of your death." So, the Lord blamed Cain, because he had killed Abel, and He made him a fugitive on the earth because of the blood of his brother, and He cursed him on the earth.

Because of this it is written on the heavenly tablets, "Cursed is he who kills his neighbor treacherously, and let all who have seen and heard say, 'So be it', and the man who has seen and not reported it, let him be accursed as the one committing it." For this reason the angels announce when they come before the Lord our God all the sin that is committed in heaven and on earth, and in light and in darkness, and everywhere.

It was in this day that God prepared a place for the dead of man, for until now no one had died that was a living soul. And Enoch would later prophesy about this place. And Enoch, when he was taken up to God saw there was a place and in it four hollow places, deep and wide and very smooth. How smooth are the hollow places and they looked deep and dark. And he asked the angel regarding these places.

Then Raphael, one of the holy angels, answered and said, "These hollow places have been created for this very purpose, that the spirits of the souls of the dead should be gathered here, that all the souls of the children of men should be brought together here. And these places have been made to receive them until the day of their judgment and until the period appointed, until the great judgment comes on them."

Enoch saw the spirit of a dead man, and his voice went out to heaven and made petitions. Raphael the angel said to him, "This spirit petitions heaven." Enoch said, "Whose voice goes up and petitions heaven?"

Raphael said, "This is the spirit which went out from Abel, whom his brother Cain slew, and he makes his suit against him until his offspring is destroyed from the face of the earth, and his offspring are annihilated from among the children of men."

And Adam and his wife mourned for Abel four weeks of years, and in the fourth year of the fifth week they became joyful, and Adam knew his wife again, and she gave birth to a son, and he called his name Seth, for he said "God has raised up a second offspring to us on the earth instead of Abel; for Cain killed him."

In the sixth week he begat his daughter Azura. And Cain took Awan his sister to be his wife and she gave birth to Enoch at the close of the fourth jubilee. In the first year of the first week of the fifth jubilee, houses were built on the earth, and Cain built a city, and called its name after the name of his son Enoch.

Adam knew Eve his wife and she gave birth to a total of nine sons. In the fifth week of the fifth jubilee Seth took Azura his sister to be his wife, and in the fourth year of the sixth week she gave birth to Enos.

He began to call on the name of the Lord on the earth. In the seventh jubilee in the third week Enos took Noam his sister to be his wife, and she gave birth to a son in the third year of the fifth week, and he called his name Kenan.

At the close of the eighth jubilee Kenan took Mualeleth his sister to be his wife, and she gave birth to a son in the ninth jubilee, in the first week in the third year of this week, and he called his name Mahalalel.

In the second week of the tenth jubilee Mahalalel took to him to wife Dinah, the daughter of Barakiel the daughter of his father's brother, and she gave birth to a son in the third week in the sixth year. And he called his name Jared, for in his days the angels of the Lord descended on the earth, those who are named the Watchers, that they should instruct the children of men, and that they should do judgment and uprightness on the earth.

And it came to pass when the children of men had multiplied that in those days were born to them beautiful and fair daughters. And when men began to multiply on the face of the earth, and daughters were born unto them, the sons of God saw the daughters of men that they were fair; and they took them wives of all which they chose. And the Lord said, "My spirit shall not always strive with man, for that he also is flesh yet his days shall be an hundred and twenty years."

And the angels, the sons of heaven, saw and lusted after them, and said to one another, "Come, let us choose us wives from among the children of men and have children with them." And Semjaza, who was their leader, said to them, "I fear you will not agree to do this deed and I alone shall have to pay the penalty of this great sin." And they all answered him and said, "Let us all swear an oath, and all bind ourselves by mutual curses so we will not abandon this plan but to do this thing."

Then they all swore together and bound themselves by mutual curses. And they were in all two hundred who descended in the days of Jared on the summit of Mount Hermon, and they called it Mount Hermon, because they had sworn and bound themselves by mutual curses on the act.

I will therefore put you in remembrance, though you once knew this, how that the Lord, having saved the people out of the land of Egypt, afterward destroyed them that believed not. And the angels who kept not their first estate, but left their own habitation, he had reserved in everlasting chains under darkness unto the judgment of the great day. And these are the names of their leaders: Samlazaz, their leader, Araklba, Rameel, Kokablel, Tamlel, Ramlel, Danel, Ezeqeel, Baraqijal, *(Author's note: Samlazaz could be another spelling of Semjaza, and possibly be the same entity.)*, Asael, Amaros, Batarel, Ananel, Zaqiel, Samsapeel, Satarel, Turel, Jomjael, Sariel. These are their chiefs of tens.

And all of them together went and took wives for themselves, each choosing one for himself, and they began to go in to them and to defile themselves with sex with them.

There were giants in the earth in those days; and also after that, when the sons of God came in unto the daughters of men, and they gave birth to children for them, the same became mighty men which were of old, men of renown (of legend).

And God saw that the wickedness of man was great in the earth, and that every imagination of the thoughts of his heart was only evil continually. And it repented the Lord that he had made man on the earth, and it grieved him at his heart.

And the angels began to teach the men of earth charms and spells, and the cutting of roots, and made them acquainted with plants.

And the women became pregnant, and they gave birth to large giants, whose height was three thousand cubits (ells). The giants consumed all the work and toil of men. And when men could no longer sustain them, the giants turned against them and devoured mankind.

And they began to sin against birds, and beasts, and reptiles, and fish, and to devour one another's flesh, and drank the blood. Then the earth laid accusation against the lawless ones.

And Azazel taught men to make swords, and knives, and shields, and breastplates, and taught them about metals of the earth and the art of working them, and bracelets, and ornaments, and the use of antimony, and the beautifying of the eyelids, and all kinds of precious stones, and all coloring and dyes. And there was great impiety, they turned away from God, and committed fornication, and they were led astray, and became corrupt in all their ways.

Semjaza taught the casting of spells, and root-cuttings, Armaros taught counter-spells (release from spells), Baraqijal taught astrology, Kokabel taught the constellations (portents), Ezeqeel the knowledge of the clouds, Araqiel the signs of the earth, Shamsiel the signs of the sun, and Sariel the course of the moon. And as men perished, they cried, and their cry went up to heaven.

And then Michael, Uriel, Raphael, and Gabriel looked down from heaven and saw much blood being shed on the earth, and all lawlessness being done on the earth. And they said to each other: "Let the cries from the destruction of Earth ascend up to the gates of heaven." And now to you, the holy ones of heaven, the souls of men make their petition, saying, "Bring our cause before the Most High."

And they said to the Lord of the ages. "Lord of lords, God of gods, King of kings, and God of the ages, the throne of your glory endures through all the generations of the ages, and your name holy and glorious and blessed to all the ages! Which in his times he shall show, who is the blessed and only Potentate, the King of kings, and Lord of lords; Who only hath immortality, dwelling in the light which no man can approach unto; whom no man hath seen, nor can see: to whom be honor and power everlasting. Amen.

You have made all things, and you have power over all things: and all things are revealed and open in your sight, and you see all things, and nothing can hide itself from you.

Look at what Azazel has done, who hath taught all unrighteousness on earth and revealed the eternal secrets which were made and kept in heaven, which men were striving to learn: And Semjaza, who taught spells, to whom you gave authority to rule over his associates."

And it was in the hundred and thirtieth year of the life of Adam upon the earth, that he again knew Eve his wife, and she conceived and gave birth to a son and he looked like Adam, and she called his name Seth, saying, "Because God has appointed me another offspring in the place of Abel, for Cain has slain him."

And Seth lived one hundred and five years, and he begat a son; and Seth called the name of his son Enosh, saying, "Because in that time the sons of men began to reproduce, and to afflict their souls and hearts by disobeying and rebelling against God."

And it was in the days of Enosh that the sons of men continued to rebel and go contrary, against God, to increase the anger of the Lord against the sons of men.

And the sons of men went and they served other gods, and they forgot the Lord who had created them in the earth: and in those days the sons of men made images of brass and iron, wood and stone, and they bowed down and served them.

And every man made his god and they bowed down to them, and

the sons of men turned away from the Lord all the days of Enosh and his children; and the anger of the Lord was set ablaze on account of their works and abominations which they did in the earth.

And the Lord caused the waters of the river Gihon to overwhelm them, and he destroyed and consumed them, and he destroyed the third part of the earth. Notwithstanding this, the sons of men did not turn from their evil ways, and their hands were yet extended to do evil in the sight of the Lord.

And in those days there was neither sowing nor reaping in the earth; and there was no food for the sons of men and the famine was very great in those days.

And the seed (offspring) which they sowed in those days in the ground became thorns, thistles and briers; for from the days of Adam was this declaration concerning the earth, of the curse of God, which he cursed the earth, on account of the sin which Adam sinned before the Lord.

And it was when men continued to rebel and go contrary, against God, and to corrupt their ways, that the earth also became corrupt.

And Enosh lived ninety years and he begat Cainan;

And Cainan grew up and he was forty years old, and he became wise and had knowledge and skill in all wisdom, and he reigned over all the sons of men, and he led the sons of men to wisdom and knowledge; for Cainan was a very wise man and had understanding in all wisdom, and with his wisdom he ruled over spirits and demons;

And Cainan knew by his wisdom that God would destroy the sons of men for having sinned upon earth, and that the Lord would in the latter days bring upon them the waters of the flood. And in those days Cainan wrote upon tablets of stone what was to take place in the time to come, and he put them in his treasures. And Cainan reigned over the whole earth, and he turned some of the sons of men to the service of God.

And Lamech, the son of Methusael, became related to Cainan by marriage, and he took his two daughters for his wives, and Adah conceived and gave birth to a son to Lamech, and she called his name Jabal. And she again conceived and gave birth to a son, and called his name Jubal; and Zillah, her sister, was barren in those days and had no offspring. For in those days the sons of men began to trespass against God, and to transgress the commandments, which he had commanded to Adam, to be fruitful and multiply in the earth.

And some of the sons of men caused their wives to drink a potion that would render them barren, in order that they might retain their figures and therefore their beautiful appearance might not fade. And when the sons of men caused some of their wives to drink, Zillah drank with them.

And the child-bearing women appeared abominable in the sight of their husbands as widows, whilst their husbands lived, for to the barren ones only, they were attached. And in the end of days and years, when Zillah became old, the Lord opened her womb. And she conceived and had a son and she called his name Tubal Cain, saying, "After I had withered away have I obtained him from the Almighty God." And she conceived again and gave birth to a daughter, and she called her name Naamah, for she said, "After I had withered away have I obtained pleasure and delight."

And Lamech was old and advanced in years, and his eyes were dim that he could not see, and Tubal Cain, his son, was leading him into the field and Tubal Cain his son was with him, and whilst they were walking in the field, Cain the son of Adam advanced towards them; for Lamech was very old and could not see much, and Tubal Cain his son was very young.

And Tubal Cain told his father to draw his bow, and with the arrows he smote Cain, who was yet far off, and he slew him, for he appeared to them to be an animal. And the arrows entered Cain's body although he was distant from them, and he fell to the ground and died. And the Lord requited Cain's evil according to his wickedness, which he had done to his brother Abel, according to the word of the Lord which he had spoken.

And it came to pass when Cain had died, that Lamech and Tubal went to see the animal which they had slain, and they saw, and behold Cain their grandfather was fallen dead upon the earth. And Lamech was very much grieved at having done this, and in clapping his hands together he struck his son and caused his death. And the wives of Lamech heard what Lamech had done, and they sought to kill him. And the wives of Lamech hated him from that day, because he slew Cain and Tubal Cain, and the wives of Lamech separated from him, and would not hearken to him in those days.

And Lamech came to his wives, and he pressed them to listen to him about this matter. And he said to his wives Adah and Zillah, "Hear my voice O wives of Lamech, attend to my words, for now you have imagined and said that I slew a man with my wounds, and a child with my stripes for their having done no violence, but surely know that I am old and grey-headed, and that my eyes are heavy through age, and I did this thing unknowingly."

And the wives of Lamech listened to him in this matter, and they returned to him with the advice of their father Adam, but they bore no children to him from that time, knowing that God's anger was increasing in those days against the sons of men, to destroy them with the waters of the flood for their evil doings. And Mahlallel the son of Cainan lived sixty-five years and he begat Jared; and Jared lived sixty-two years and he begat Enoch.

In the eleventh jubilee Jared took to himself a wife, and her name was Baraka, the daughter of Rasujal, a daughter of his father's brother, in the fourth week of this jubilee, and she gave birth to a son in the fifth week, in the fourth year of the jubilee, and he called his name Enoch.

He was the first among men that are born on earth who learned writing and knowledge and wisdom and who wrote down the signs of heaven according to the order of their months in a book, that men might know the seasons of the years according to the order of their separate months.

He was the first to write a testimony and he testified to the sons of men among the generations of the earth, and recounted the weeks of the jubilees, and made known to them the days of the years, and set in order the months and recounted the Sabbaths of the years as we made them known to him.

And the children of the Watchers were monsters, devouring fruit, grain, animals, and men. And their appetites could never be quenched, for neither food, nor sex. And they did unspeakable acts to women, men, animals, and even birds. The offspring of spiritual creatures and earthly animals were the monsters of legends, half man – half animal.

But the fallen ones began to dream dreams and see visions. These were shadows of things to come. And one of their leaders, called Gilgamesh, desired to know the meaning of the visions, but there were none who could interpret the visions. So he sent to ask of Enoch, the wise scribe. Taking up to the air by lapping his arms like the wings of an eagle, the monster flew across desolation and desert to find Enoch. When Enoch was found and salutations made, the monster told Enoch of the visions and besought his wisdom. And Enoch interpreted the visions to mean the destruction of all Watchers, for the mercy of God had long left the Watchers because of their deeds and the spread of sin and destruction across the Earth and the abominations produced by the lusts of the Watchers and their offspring. And the Watchers and their children were frightened, for they knew their destruction was near but did not know the time or the way their life would end.

And Enoch was a righteous man who walked with God. And Enoch did not die but God took him up into heaven.

And Enoch lived sixty and five years, and begat Methuselah: And Enoch walked with God after he begat Methuselah three hundred years, and begat sons and daughters: And all the days of Enoch were three hundred sixty and five years: And Enoch walked with God: and he was not; for God took him. And Methuselah lived an hundred eighty and seven years, and begat Lamech. And Methuselah lived after he begat Lamech seven hundred eighty and two years, and begat sons and daughters: And all the days of Methuselah were nine hundred sixty and nine years: and he died. And Lamech lived an hundred eighty and two years, and begat a son: And he called his name Noah, saying, This same shall comfort us concerning our work and toil of our hands, because of the ground which the LORD hath cursed.

Then, the angels prayed to God saying, "You know all things before they come to pass, and you see these things and you have permitted them, and say nothing to us about these things. What are we to do with them about these things?"

At this time, Noah was five hundred years old, and Noah begat Shem, Ham, and Japheth.

Then said the Most High, the Great and Holy One, "Go to the son of Lamech, Uriel. Say to him: Go to Noah and tell him in my name hide yourself and reveal to him the end that is approaching; that the whole earth will be destroyed, and a flood is about to come on the whole earth, and will destroy everything on it."

"For yet seven days, and I will cause it to rain upon the earth forty days and forty nights; and every living substance that I have made will I destroy from off the face of the earth. And now instruct him as to what he must do to escape that his offspring may be preserved for all the generations of the world."

And God said unto Noah, "The end of all flesh is come before me; for the earth is filled with violence through them. And, behold, I will destroy them with the earth. Make thee an ark of gopher wood; rooms shalt thou make in the ark, and shalt pitch it within and without with pitch."

And again the Lord said to Raphael, "Bind Azazel hand and foot, and cast him into the darkness and split open the desert, which is in Dudael, and cast him in. And fill the hole by covering him rough and jagged rocks, and cover him with darkness, and let him live there for ever, and cover his face that he may not see the light."

"And on the day of the great judgment he shall be hurled into the fire. And heal the earth which the angels have ruined, and proclaim the healing of the earth, for I will restore the earth and heal the plague, that not all of the children of men may perish through all the secret things that the Watchers have disclosed and have taught their sons."

"For I reckon that the sufferings of this present time are not worthy to be compared with the glory which shall be revealed in us. For the earnest expectation of the creature waiteth for the manifestation of the sons of God. For the creature was made subject to vanity, not willingly, but by reason of him who hath subjected the same in hope; because the creature itself also shall be delivered from the bondage of corruption into the glorious liberty of the children of God."

The whole earth has been corrupted through the works that were taught by Azazel: to him ascribe ALL SIN. And all the sons of men departed from the ways of the Lord in those days as they multiplied upon the face of the earth with sons and daughters, and they taught one another their evil practices and they continued sinning against the Lord. And every man made unto himself a god, and they robbed and plundered every man his neighbor as well as his relative, and they corrupted the earth, and the earth was filled with violence.

And their judges and rulers went to the daughters of men and took their wives by force from their husbands according to their choice.

And the sons of men in those days took from the cattle of the earth, the beasts of the field and the fowls of the air, and taught the mixture of animals of one species with the other, in order therewith to provoke the Lord; and God saw the whole earth and it was corrupt, for all flesh had corrupted its ways upon earth, all men and all animals.

To Gabriel said the Lord, "Proceed against the bastards and the reprobates, and against the children of fornication and destroy the children of fornication and the children of the Watchers. Cause them to go against one another that they may destroy each other in battle: Shorten their days."

And the Lord said, "I will destroy man whom I have created from the face of the earth; both man, and beast, and the creeping thing, and the fowls of the air; for it repenteth me that I have made them."

And the Lord said to Michael, "Go, bind Semjaza and his team who have associated with women and have defiled themselves in all their uncleanness. When their sons have slain one another, and they have seen the destruction of their beloved ones, bind them fast for seventy generations under the hills of the earth, until the day of the consummation of their judgment and until the eternal judgment is accomplished."

(Author's note: 70 generations of 500 years = 3500 years.)

"In those days they shall be led off to the abyss of fire and to the torment and the prison in which they shall be confined for ever. Then Semjaza shall be burnt up with the condemned and they will be destroyed, having been bound together with them to the end of all generations. Destroy all the spirits of lust and the children of the Watchers, because they have wronged mankind."

For God spared not the angels that sinned, but cast them down to hell, and delivered them into chains of darkness, to be reserved unto judgment.

"Destroy all wrong from the face of the earth and let every evil work come to an end and let (the earth be planted with righteousness) the plant of righteousness and truth appear (messiah); and it shall prove a blessing, the works of righteousness and truth shall be planted in truth and joy for evermore."

And the Lord said, "I will destroy man whom I have created from the face of the earth; both man, and beast, and the creeping thing, and the fowls of the air; for it repenteth me that I have made them. And then shall all the righteous survive, and shall live until they beget thousands of children, and all the days of their youth and their old age shall they complete in peace. While the earth remaineth, seedtime and harvest, and cold and heat, and summer and winter, and day and night shall not cease."

And God blessed Noah and his sons, and said unto them, "Be fruitful, and multiply, and replenish the earth. And then shall the whole earth be tilled in righteousness. And all desirable trees shall be planted on it, and they shall plant vines on it. And the vine which they plant shall yield fruit in abundance, and as for all the seed which is sown, each measurement (of it) shall bear a thousand, and each measurement of olives shall yield ten presses of oil. You shall cleanse the earth from all oppression, and from all unrighteousness, and from all sin, and from all godlessness, and all the uncleanness that is brought on the earth you shall destroy from off the earth."

Because of these three things came the flood on the earth, namely, the fornication that the Watchers committed against the law of their ordinances when they went whoring after the daughters of men, and took themselves wives of all they chose, and they made the beginning of uncleanness. And they begat sons, the Nephilim, and they were all dissimilar, and they devoured one another, and the Giants killed the Naphil, and the Naphil killed the Eljo, and the Eljo killed mankind, and one man killed one another.

Every one committed himself to crime and injustice and to shed much blood, and the earth was filled with sin. After this they sinned against the beasts and birds, and all that moved and walked on the earth, and much blood was shed on the earth, and men continually desired only what was useless and evil.

And the Lord destroyed everything from the face of the earth. Because of the wickedness of their deeds, and because of the blood they had shed over all the earth, He destroyed everything.

And against the angels whom He had sent on the earth, He had boiling anger, and He gave commandment to root them out of all their dominion, and He commanded us to bind them in the depths of the earth, and look, they are bound in the middle of the earth, and are kept separate. And against their sons went out a command from His mouth that they should be killed with the sword, and be left under heaven.

He sent His sword into their presence that each should kill his neighbor, and they began to kill each other until they all fell by the sword and were destroyed from the earth. And their fathers were witnesses of their destruction, and after this they were bound in the depths of the earth forever, until the day of the great condemnation, when judgment is executed on all those who have corrupted their ways and their works before the Lord.

He destroyed all wherever they were, and there was not one left of them whom He judged according to all their wickedness. Through His work He made a new and righteous nature, so that they should not sin in their whole nature forever, but should be all righteous each in his own way always.

The judgment of all is ordained and written on the heavenly tablets in righteousness, even the judgment of all who depart from the path that is ordained for them to walk; and if they do not walk it, judgment is written down for every creature and for every kind. There is nothing in heaven or on earth, or in light or in darkness, or in the abode of the dead or in the depth, or in the place of darkness that is not judged. All their judgments are ordained and written and engraved.

He will judge all, the great according to his greatness, and the small according to his smallness, and each according to his way. He is not one who will regard the position of any person, nor is He one who will receive gifts, if He says that He will execute judgment on each. If one gave everything that is on the earth, He will not regard the gifts or the person of any, nor accept anything at his hands, for He is a righteous judge. Of the children of Israel it has been written and ordained, if they turn to him in righteousness He will forgive all their transgressions and pardon all their sins. It is written and ordained that He will show mercy to all who turn from all their guilt once each year.

And as for all those who corrupted their ways and their thoughts before the flood, no person was acceptable to God except Noah. His sons were saved in deference to him, and these God kept from the waters of the flood on his account; for Noah's heart was righteous in all his ways. He upheld the laws and did as God commanded him and he had not departed from anything that was ordained for him.

The Lord said that he would destroy everything on the earth, both men and cattle, and beasts, and birds of the air, and that which moves on the earth. And He commanded Noah to make an ark, so that he might save himself from the waters of the flood. And Noah made the ark in all respects as He commanded him, in the twenty-seventh jubilee of years, in the fifth week in the fifth year on the new moon of the first month. He entered in the sixth year of it, in the second month, on the new moon of the second month, until the sixteenth; and he entered, and all that we brought to him, into the ark, and the Lord closed it from the outside on the seventeenth evening.

And the Lord opened seven floodgates of heaven, and He opened the mouths of the fountains of the great deep, seven mouths in number. And the floodgates began to pour down water from the heaven forty days and forty closets (nights). And the fountains of the deep also sent up waters, until the whole world was full of water.

The waters increased on the earth, by fifteen cubits (a cubit is about 18 inches) the waters rose above all the high mountains. And the ark was lifted up from the earth. And it moved on the face of the waters.

And the water covered the face of the earth five months, which is one hundred and fifty days. And all flesh was destroyed, but the spirits of the evil ones were not destroyed. Having sought out the flesh of animals in which to live after their bodies were killed, the spirits of the giants and the children of the Watchers escaped and waited.

And the ark went and rested on the top of Lubar, one of the mountains of Ararat. On the new moon in the fourth month the fountains of the great deep were closed and the floodgates of heaven were restrained; and on the new moon of the seventh month all the mouths of the bottomless gulfs of the earth were opened, and the water began to flow down into the deep below. On the new moon of the tenth month the tops of the mountains were seen, and on the new moon of the first month the earth became visible. The waters disappeared from the earth in the fifth week in the seventh year of it, and on the seventeenth day in the second month the earth was dry.

On the twenty-seventh of it he opened the ark, and sent out beasts, and cattle, and birds, and every moving thing. And the spirits of the evil ones began to inhabit animals and men once again.

And it would come to pass in the future that there would arise war at Gezer with the Philistines; at which time Sibbechai the Hushathite would kill Sippai, who was of the children of the giant, and they were subdued. And there would be war again with the Philistines; and Elhanan the son of Jair would slay Lahmi the brother of Goliath the Gittite, whose spear staff was like a weaver's beam. And yet again there was war at Gath, where there was a man of great stature, whose fingers and toes were four and twenty, six on each hand, and six on each foot and he also was the son of the giant. These would be born unto the giant in Gath, being descended from the Watchers; and they would fall by the hand of David, and by the hand of his servants. Thus the evil of the Watchers would continue to plague the children of God.

On the new moon of the third month Noah went out of the ark, and built an altar on that mountain. And he made atonement for the earth, and took a kid and made atonement by its blood for all the guilt of the earth; for every thing that had been on it had been destroyed, except those that were in the ark with Noah.

He placed the fat of it on the altar, and he took an ox, and a goat, and a sheep and kids, and salt, and a turtle-dove, and the young of a dove, and placed a burnt sacrifice on the altar, and poured on it an offering mingled with oil, and sprinkled wine and frankincense over everything, and caused a good and pleasing odor to arise, acceptable before the Lord.

And the Lord smelled the good and pleasing odor, and He made a covenant with Noah that there should not be any more floods to destroy the earth; that all the days of the earth seed-time and harvest should never cease; cold and heat, and summer and winter, and day and night should not change their order, nor cease forever.

"Increase and multiply on the earth, and become many, and be a blessing on it. I will inspire the fear of you and the dread of you in everything that is on earth and in the sea." And the earth was cleaned of the sins of the flesh, but spirits of the evil Watchers and their accursed offspring cannot die.

In the twenty-ninth jubilee, in the beginning of first week, Arpachshad took to himself a wife and her name was Rasu'eja, the daughter of Susan, the daughter of Elam, and she gave birth to a son in the third year in this week, and he called his name Kainam. The son grew, and his father taught him writing, and he went to seek for himself a place where he might seize a city for himself. He found writing which former generations had carved on a rock, and he read what was on it, and he transcribed it and sinned because of it, for it contained the teaching of the Watchers, which they had used to observe the omens of the sun and moon and stars in all the signs of heaven.

He wrote it down and said nothing of it, for he was afraid to speak to Noah about it or he would be angry with him because of it. In the third week of this jubilee the unclean demons began to lead astray the children of the sons of Noah, and to make them sin and to destroy them.

The sons of Noah came to Noah their father, and they told him about the demons that were leading astray and blinding and slaying his sons' sons.

And Noah said, "I see the demons have begun their seductions against you and against your children and now I fear on your behalf, that after my death you will shed the blood of men on the earth, and that you, too, will be destroyed from the face of the earth.

"For whoever sheds man's blood, and who ever eats the blood of any flesh, shall all be destroyed from the earth."

And he prayed before the Lord his God, and said, "God of the spirits of all flesh, who have shown mercy to me and have spared me and my sons from the waters of the flood, and have not caused me to die as You did the sons of perdition; For your grace has been great toward me, and great has been your mercy to my soul."

"Let your grace be lifted up on my sons, and do not let the wicked spirits rule over them or they will destroy them from the earth. But bless me and my sons, so that we may increase and multiply and replenish the earth. You know how your Watchers, the fathers of these spirits, acted in my day, and as for these spirits which are living, imprison them and hold them fast in the place of condemnation, and let them not bring destruction on the sons of your servant, my God; for these are like cancer and are created in order to destroy.

Let them not rule over the spirits of the living; for You alone can exercise dominion over them. And let them not have power over the sons of the righteous from now and forever." And the Lord our God commanded the angels to bind all of them.

And the Watchers came to Enoch, whom God had taken up into heaven, and begged him to intercede before God on their behalf.

Then God answered and said, "No request that the Watchers, or their children make of you shall be granted them on their behalf; for they hope to live an eternal life, and that each one of them will live five hundred years."

And God answered and said to Enoch, "Do not be afraid, Enoch, you righteous man and scribe of righteousness. Approach and hear my voice. Go and say to the Watchers of heaven, for whom you have come to intercede: You should intercede for men, and not men for you. Why and for what cause have you left the high, holy, and eternal heaven, and had sex with women, and defiled yourselves with the daughters of men and taken to yourselves wives, and done like the children of earth, and begotten giants (as your) sons? Though you were holy, spiritual, living the eternal life, you have defiled yourselves with the blood of women, and have begotten children with the blood of flesh, and, as the children of men, you have lusted after flesh and blood like those who die and are killed.

This is why I have given men wives that they might impregnate them, and have children by them, that deeds might continue on the earth. But you were formerly spiritual, living the eternal life, and immortal for all generations of the world. Therefore I have not appointed wives for you. You are spiritual beings of heaven, and in heaven was your dwelling place. Only after death will man know what you have known.

"For the children of this world marry, and are given in marriage: But they which shall be accounted worthy to obtain that world, and the resurrection from the dead, neither marry, nor are given in marriage, neither can they die any more. For they are equal unto the angels, and are the children of God, being the children of the resurrection."

And now, the giants, who are produced from the spirits and flesh, shall be called evil spirits on the earth, and shall live on the earth. Evil spirits have come out from their bodies because they are born from men and from the holy Watchers, their beginning is of primal origin, and they shall be called spirits of the evil ones. As for the spirits of heaven, in heaven shall be their dwelling, but as for the spirits of the earth which were born on the earth, on the earth shall be their dwelling.

And the spirits of the giants afflict, oppress, destroy, attack, war, destroy, and cause trouble on the earth. Their spirits take no food, but do not hunger or thirst. They cause offences but are not seen. And these spirits shall rise up against the children of men and against the women, because they have proceeded from them in the days of the slaughter and destruction.

And at the death of the giants, spirits will go out and shall destroy without incurring judgment. Coming from their bodies, their flesh shall be destroy until the day of the consummation, the great judgment in which the age shall be consummated, over the Watchers and the godless, and shall be wholly consummated.

These evil spirits shall torment men without restraint, inhabiting animals and possessing men until the days of the Messiah come.

And now as to the Watchers who have sent you to intercede for them, who had been in heaven before, (Say to them), "You were in heaven, but all the mysteries of heaven had not been revealed to you, and you knew worthless ones, and these in the hardness of your hearts you have made known to the women, and through these mysteries women and men work much evil on earth."

Say to them therefore, "You have no peace." The chief of the spirits, Mastema (Satan), came and said, "Lord, Creator, let some of them remain before me, and let them listen to my voice, and do all that I shall say to them; for if some of them are not left to me, I shall not be able to execute the power of my will on the sons of men, for these are for corruption and leading astray before my judgment, for great is the wickedness of the sons of men."

He said, "Let one-tenth of them remain before him, and let nine-tenths of them descend into the place of condemnation."

Then God commanded one of the angels to teach Noah all their medicines, for He knew that the Watchers would not walk in uprightness, nor strive in righteousness.

The angels did according to all His words. Then they bound all the malignant evil ones in the place of condemnation and a tenth part of them we left that they might be subject in the presence of Satan on the earth. The angels explained to Noah all the medicines of their diseases, together with their seductions, how he might heal them with herbs of the earth. Noah wrote down all things in a book as they instructed him concerning every kind of medicine. Thus the evil spirits were precluded from hurting the sons of Noah.

But, the sons of Noah began to war with each other, to take captives and kill each other, and to shed the blood of men on the earth, and to eat blood, and to build strong cities, and walls, and towers, and individuals began to exalt themselves above the nation, and to establish kingdoms, and to go to war, people against people, and nation against nation, and city against city, and all began to do evil, and to acquire arms, and to teach their sons war, and they began to capture cities, and to sell male and female slaves.

In the three and thirtieth jubilee, in the first year in the second week, Peleg took to himself a wife, whose name was Lomna the daughter of Sina'ar, and she gave birth to a son for him in the fourth year of this week, and he called his name Reu, for he said, "Look the children of men have become evil because they conceived building a city and a tower in the land of Shinar for an evil purpose." For they departed from the land of Ararat eastward to Shinar, for in his days they built the city and the tower, saying, "Let us build this now so that we may rise into heaven."

And in these days King Nimrod reigned securely, and all the earth was under his control, and all the earth was of one tongue and words of union.

And all the princes of Nimrod and his great men took counsel together; Phut, Mitzraim, Cush and Canaan with their families, and they said to each other, "Come let us build ourselves a city and in it a strong tower, and its top reaching heaven, and we will make ourselves famed, so that we may reign upon the whole world, in order that the evil of our enemies may cease from us, that we may reign mightily over them, and that we may not become scattered over the earth on account of their wars."

And they all went before the king, and they told the king these words, and the king agreed with them in this affair, and he did so.

And all the families assembled consisting of about six hundred thousand men, and they went to seek an extensive piece of ground to build the city and the tower, and they sought in the whole earth and they found none like one valley at the east of the land of Shinar, about two days' walk, and they journeyed there and they lived there. And they began to make bricks and burn fires to build the city and the tower that they imagined to complete. And the building of the tower was to them a transgression and a sin, and they began to build it, and whilst they were building against the Lord God of heaven, they imagined in their hearts to war against him and to ascend into heaven.

They began to build, and in the fourth week they made brick with fire, and the bricks served them for stone, and the clay with which they cemented them together was asphalt which comes out of the sea, and out of the fountains of water in the land of Shinar. They built it, forty-three years were they building it. Its breadth was 203 bricks, and the height of a brick was the third of one; its height amounted to 8149.5 feet (5433 cubits) and 8 inches (2 palms,) and the extent of one wall was thirteen times 600 feet and of the other thirty times 600 feet.

And all these people and all the families divided themselves in three parts. The first said, "We will ascend into heaven and fight against him;" the second said, "We will ascend to heaven and place our own gods there and serve them;" and the third part said, "We will ascend to heaven and strike him with bows and spears;" and God knew all their works and all their evil thoughts, and he saw the city and the tower which they were building.

And when they were building they built themselves a great city and a very high and strong tower; and on account of its height the mortar and bricks did not reach the builders in their ascent to it, until those who went up had completed a full year, and after that, they reached to the builders and gave them the mortar and the bricks; thus was it done daily. And behold these ascended and others descended the whole day; and if a brick should fall from their hands and get broken, they would all weep over it, and if a man fell and died, none of them would look at him.

And the Lord knew their thoughts, and it came to pass when they were building they cast the arrows toward the heavens, and all the arrows fell upon them filled with blood, and when they saw them they said to each other, "Certainly we have slain all those that are in heaven." For this was from the Lord in order to cause them to err, and in order to destroy them from off the face of the earth.

And they built the tower and the city, and they did this thing daily until many days and years were elapsed.

And the Lord our God said to the angels, "Look, they are one people, and they begin to do this, and now nothing will be withheld from them. Let us go down and confound their language, that they may not understand one another's speech, and they may be dispersed into cities and nations, and they will not be in agreement together with one purpose until the Day of Judgment."

And God said to the seventy angels who stood foremost before him, to those who were near to him, saying, "Come let us descend and confuse their tongues, that one man shall not understand the language of his neighbor." And they did so.

And from that day following, they forgot each man his neighbor's tongue, and they could not understand to speak in one tongue, and when the builder took from the hands of his neighbor lime or stone which he did not order, the builder would cast it away and throw it upon his neighbor, that he would die. And they did so many days, and they killed many of them in this manner.

And the Lord struck the three divisions that were there, and he punished them according to their works and designs. Those who said, "We will ascend to heaven and serve our gods," became like apes and elephants; and those who said, "We will strike the heaven with arrows," the Lord killed them, one man through the hand of his neighbor; and the third division of those who said, "We will ascend to heaven and fight against him," the Lord scattered them throughout the earth.

And those who were left amongst them, when they knew and understood the evil which was coming upon them, they turned away from the building, and they also became scattered upon the face of the whole earth. And they ceased building the city and the tower; therefore he called that place Babel, for there the Lord confounded the language of the whole earth; behold it was at the east of the land of Shinar.

And the Lord descended, and the angels descended with him to see the city and the tower that the children of men had built. He confounded their language, and they no longer understood one another's speech, and they then ceased to build the city and the tower. For this reason the whole land of Shinar is called Babel, because the Lord confounded all the language of the children of men there, and from that place they were dispersed into their cities, each according to his language and his nation.

Then, the Lord sent a mighty wind against the tower and it fell to the earth, and behold it was between Asshur and Babylon in the land of Shinar, and they called its name "Overthrow." And as to the tower which the sons of men built, the earth opened its mouth and swallowed up one third part thereof, and a fire also descended from heaven and burned another third, and the other third is left to this day, and it is of that part which was aloft, and its circumference is three days' walk. And many of the sons of men died in that tower, a people without number.

In the fourth week in the first year in the beginning of it in the four and thirtieth jubilee, were they dispersed from the land of Shinar. Ham and his sons went into the land that he was to occupy, which he acquired as his portion in the land of the south. Ur, the son of Kesed, built the city of Ara (Ur?) of the Chaldees, and called its name after his own name and the name of his father.

And they made themselves molten images, and they worshipped the idols and the molten image they had made for themselves, and they began to make graven images and unclean and shadowy presence, and malevolent and malicious spirits assisted and seduced them into committing transgression and uncleanness.

Prince Mastema exerted himself to do all this, and he sent out other spirits, which were put under his control, to do all manner of wrong and sin, and all manner of transgression, to corrupt and destroy, and to shed blood on the earth.

For this reason he called the name of Seroh, Serug, for every one turned to do all manner of sin and transgression.

He grew up, and dwelt in Ur of the Chaldees, near to the father of his wife's mother, and he worshipped idols, and he took to himself a wife in the thirty-sixth jubilee, in the fifth week, in the first year of it, and her name was Melka, the daughter of Kaber, the daughter of his father's brother.

She gave birth to Nahor, in the first year of this week, and he grew and dwelt in Ur of the Chaldees, and his father taught him the sciences of the Chaldees to divine and conjure, according to the signs of heaven. In the thirty-seventh jubilee in the sixth week, in the first year of it, he took to himself a wife, and her name was 'Ijaska, the daughter of Nestag of the Chaldees. And she gave birth to Terah in the seventh year of this week.

Prince Mastema (Satan) sent ravens and birds to devour the seed that was sown in the land, in order to destroy the land, and rob the children of men of their labors. Before they could plow in the seed, the ravens picked it from the surface of the ground. This is why he called his name Terah because the ravens and the birds reduced them to destitution and devoured their seed.

The years began to be barren because of the birds, and they devoured all the fruit from the trees, it was only with great effort that they could harvest a little fruit from the earth in their days.

In the seventh year of this week the wife of Terah gave birth to a son, and called his name Abram, by the name of the father of his mother, for he had died before his daughter had conceived a son. And the child began to understand the errors of the earth that all went astray after graven images and after uncleanness. His father taught him writing, and he was two weeks of years old when he separated himself from his father, that he might not worship idols with him. He began to pray to the Creator of all things that He might spare him from the errors of the children of men, and that his portion should not fall into error after uncleanness and vileness.

The time came for the sowing of seed in the land, and they all went out together to protect their seed against the ravens, and Abram, a lad of fourteen, went out with those that went. A cloud of ravens came to devour the seed and Abram ran to meet them before they settled on the ground, and cried to them before they settled on the ground to devour the seed, and said, "Descend not, return to the place from where you came," and they began to turn back. And he caused the clouds of ravens to turn back that day seventy times, and of all the ravens throughout all the land where Abram was there settled not so much as one.

All who were with him throughout all the land saw him cry out, and all the ravens turn back, and his name became great in all the land of the Chaldees. There came to him this year all those that wished to sow, and he went with them until the time of sowing ceased, and they sowed their land, and that year they brought enough grain home to eat and they were satisfied.

In the first year of the fifth week Abram taught those who made implements for oxen, the artificers in wood, and they made a vessel above the ground, facing the frame of the plow, in order to put the seed in it, and the seed fell down from it on the share of the plow, and was hidden in the earth, and they no longer feared the ravens. After this manner they made vessels above the ground on all the frames of the plows, and they sowed and tilled all the land, according as Abram commanded them, and they no longer feared the birds.

In the sixth week, in the seventh year of it, Abram said to Terah his father, "Father!" And Terah said, "Look, here am I, my son." He said to his father, "What help and profit have we from those idols which you worship, and in the presence of which you bow yourself? There is no spirit in them. They are dumb forms, and they mislead the heart. Do not worship them. Worship the God of heaven, who causes the rain and the dew to fall on the earth and does everything on the earth, and has created everything by His word, and all life is from His presence.

Why do you worship things that have no spirit in them? For they are the work of men's hands, and you bear them on your shoulders, and you have no help from them, but they are a great cause of shame to those who make them, and they mislead the heart of those who worship them. Do not worship them."

His father replied, "I also know it, my son, but what shall I do with a people who have made me serve them? If I tell them the truth, they will kill me, because their soul clings to them so they worship them and honor them. Keep silent, my son, or they will kill you." And these words he spoke to his two brothers, and they were angry with him and he kept silent.

In the fortieth jubilee, in the second week, in the seventh year of it, Abram took to himself a wife, and her name was Sarai, the daughter of his father, and she became his wife. Haran, his brother, took to himself a wife in the third year of the third week, and she gave birth to a son in the seventh year of this week, and he called his name Lot. Nahor, his brother, took to himself a wife. In the sixtieth year of the life of Abram, that is, in the fourth week, in the fourth year of it, Abram arose in the night and burned the house of the idols, and he burned all that was in the house and no man knew it.

And they arose and sought to save their gods from the fire. Haran hasted to save them, but the fire flamed over him, and he was burnt in the fire, and he died in Ur of the Chaldees before Terah his father, and they buried him in Ur of the Chaldees. Terah went out from Ur of the Chaldees, he and his sons, to go into the land of Lebanon and into the land of Canaan, and he dwelt in the land of Haran, and Abram dwelt with Terah his father in Haran two weeks of years.

In the sixth week, in the fifth year of it, Abram sat up all night on the new moon of the seventh month to observe the stars from the evening to the morning, in order to see what would be the character of the year with regard to the rains, and he was alone as he sat and observed. And a word came into his heart and he said, "All the signs of the stars, and the signs of the moon and of the sun are all in the hand of the Lord. Why do I search them out? If He desires, He causes it to rain, morning and evening, and if He desires, He withholds it, and all things are in his hand." He prayed in the night and said, "My God, God Most High, You alone are my God, and You and your dominion have I chosen.

And You have created all things, and all things are the work of Your hands. Deliver me from the hands of evil spirits who have dominion over the thoughts of men's hearts, and let them not lead me astray from You, my God.

And establish me and my offspring forever so that we do not go astray from now and forever." He said, "Shall I return to Ur of the Chaldees who are trying to find me? Should I return to them? Am I to remain here in this place? The right path is before You. Make it prosper in the hands of your servant that he may fulfill it and that I may not walk in the deceitfulness of my heart, O my God." He stopped speaking and stopped praying.

Then the word of the Lord was sent to him through an angel, saying, "Get out of your country, and from your kindred and from the house of your father and go to a land which I will show you, and I shall make you a great and numerous nation. And I will bless you and I will make your name great, and you will be blessed in the earth, and in You shall all families of the earth be blessed, and I will bless them that bless you, and curse them that curse you. I will be a God to you and your son, and to your son's son, and to all your offspring, fear not, from now on and to all generations of the earth I am your God."

The Lord God said to the angel, "Open his mouth and his ears, that he may hear and speak with his mouth, with the language which has been revealed." For it had ceased from the mouths of all the children of men from the day of the overthrow of Babel. And the angel opened his mouth, and his ears and his lips, and the angel began to speak with him in Hebrew in the tongue of the creation. He took the books of his fathers, and these were written in Hebrew, and he transcribed them, and he began from then on to study them, and the angel made known to him that which he could not understand, and he studied them during the six rainy months.

In the seventh year of the sixth week he spoke to his father and informed him that he would leave Haran to go into the land of Canaan to see it and return to him. Terah his father said to him, "Go in peace. May the eternal God make your path straight. And the Lord be with you, and protect you from all evil, and grant to you grace, mercy, and favor before those who see you, and may none of the children of men have power over you to harm you. Go in peace. If you see a land pleasant to your eyes to dwell in, then arise and take me with you and take Lot with you, the son of Haran your brother as your own son, the Lord be with you. Nahor your brother leave with me until you return in peace, and we go with you all together."

And Peleg the son of Eber died in those days, in the forty-eighth year of the life of Abram son of Terah, and all the days of Peleg were two hundred and thirty-nine years.

Abram journeyed from Haran, and he took Sarai, his wife, and Lot, his brother Haran's son and they went to the land of Canaan, and he came into Asshur, and proceeded to Shechem, and dwelt near a tall oak. He saw the land was very pleasant from the border of Hamath to the tall oak. The Lord said to him, "To you and to your offspring I will give this land." He built an altar there, and he offered on it a burnt sacrifice to the Lord, who had appeared to him.

He left that place and went to the mountain Bethel on the west and Ai on the east, and pitched his tent there. He saw the land was very wide and good, and everything grew on it, vines, and figs, and pomegranates, oaks, and ilexes, and turpentine and oil trees, and cedars and cypresses, and date trees, and all trees of the field, and there was water on the mountains. And he blessed the Lord who had led him out of Ur of the Chaldees, and had brought him to this land.

And God established the covenant of circumcision with Abraham and said, "Every one that is born, the flesh of whose foreskin is not circumcised on the eighth day, does not belong to the children of the covenant which the Lord made with Abraham, but instead they belong to the children of destruction. Nor is there any other sign on him that he is the Lord's, but he is destined to be destroyed and killed from the earth, and to be rooted out of the earth, for he has broken the covenant of the Lord our God. All the angels of the presence (of the Lord) and all the angels of sanctification have been created already circumcised from the day of their creation, and before the angels of the presence (of the Lord) and the angels of sanctification He has sanctified Israel, that they should be with Him and with His holy angels.

Command the children of Israel and let them observe the sign of this covenant for their generations as an eternal law, and they will not be rooted out of the land. For the command is ordained for a covenant, that they should observe it forever among all the children of Israel. For Ishmael and his sons and his brothers, and Esau, the Lord did not cause them to come to Him, and he did not choose them. Although they are the children of Abraham, He knew them, but He chose Israel to be His people.

He sanctified them, and gathered them from among all the children of men; for there are many nations and many peoples, and all are

His, and over all nations He has placed spirits in authority to lead them astray from Him. But over Israel He did not appoint any angel or spirit, for He alone is their ruler, and He will preserve them and require them at the hand of His angels and His spirits, and at the hand of all His powers in order that He may preserve them and bless them, that they may be His and He may be theirs from now on forever.

I announce to you that the children of Israel will not keep true to this law, and they will not circumcise their sons according to all this law; for in the flesh of their circumcision they will omit this circumcision of their sons, and all of the sons of Beliar will leave their sons uncircumcised as they were born. Because of this, the Lord will be angry.

There will be great wrath from the Lord against the children of Israel because they have forsaken His covenant and turned aside from His word, and provoked (God) and blasphemed, because they do not observe the ordinance of this law; for they have treated their genitalia like the Gentiles, so that they may be removed and rooted out of the land. And there will no more be pardon or forgiveness to them for all the sin of this eternal error."

Then, in the days of King Saul, the spirits of the evil ones, the sons of the Watchers inhabited the people and animals of the land of Amalek. And God sent the prophet Samuel to speak to the king. Samuel said unto Saul, "The Lord sent me to anoint thee to be king over his people, over Israel; now therefore hearken thou unto the voice of the words of the Lord."

Thus saith the Lord of hosts, "I remember that which Amalek did to Israel, how he laid wait for him in the way, when he came up from Egypt. Now go and smite Amalek, and utterly destroy all that they have, and spare them not; but slay both man and woman, infant and suckling, ox and sheep, camel and ass." And Saul gathered the people together, and numbered them in Telaim, two hundred thousand footmen, and ten thousand men of Judah.

And Saul came to a city of Amalek, and laid wait in the valley. And Saul said unto the Kenites, "Go, depart, get you down from among the Amalekites, lest I destroy you with them, for ye shewed kindness to all the children of Israel, when they came up out of Egypt." So the Kenites departed from among the Amalekites. And Saul smote the Amalekites from Havilah until thou comest to Shur, that is over against Egypt. And he took Agag the king of the Amalekites alive, and utterly destroyed all the people with the edge of the sword.

But Saul and the people spared Agag, and the best of the sheep, and of the oxen, and of the fatlings, and the lambs, and all that was good, and would not utterly destroy them, but every thing that was vile and refuse, that they destroyed utterly.

Then came the word of the Lord unto Samuel, saying, "It repenteth me that I have set up Saul to be king, for he is turned back from following me, and hath not performed my commandments." And it grieved Samuel; and he cried unto the Lord all night. And when Samuel rose early to meet Saul in the morning, and it was told Samuel, "Saul came to Carmel, and, behold, he set him up a place, and is gone about, and passed on, and gone down to Gilgal."

And Samuel came to Saul and Saul said unto him, "Blessed be thou of the Lord, I have performed the commandment of the Lord." And Samuel said, "What meaneth then this bleating of the sheep in mine ears, and the lowing of the oxen which I hear?"

And Saul said, "They have brought them from the Amalekites, for the people spared the best of the sheep and of the oxen, to sacrifice unto the Lord thy God; and the rest we have utterly destroyed." Then Samuel said unto Saul, "Stay, and I will tell thee what the Lord hath said to me this night." And Saul said unto him, "Say on." And Samuel said, "When thou wast little in thine own sight, wast thou not made the head of the tribes of Israel, and the Lord anointed thee king over Israel?"

"And the Lord sent thee on a journey, and said, 'Go and utterly destroy the sinners the Amalekites, and fight against them until they be consumed.' Wherefore then didst thou not obey the voice of the Lord, but didst fly upon the spoil, and didst evil in the sight of the Lord?"

And Saul said unto Samuel, "Yea, I have obeyed the voice of the Lord, and have gone the way which the Lord sent me, and have brought Agag the king of Amalek, and have utterly destroyed the Amalekites. But the people took of the spoil, sheep and oxen, the chief of the things which should have been utterly destroyed, to sacrifice unto the Lord thy God in Gilgal."

And Samuel said, "Hath the Lord as great delight in burnt offerings and sacrifices, as in obeying the voice of the Lord? Behold, to obey is better than sacrifice, and to hearken than the fat of rams. For rebellion is as the sin of witchcraft, and stubbornness is as iniquity and idolatry. Because thou hast rejected the word of the Lord, he hath also rejected thee from being king."

And Saul said unto Samuel, "I have sinned for I have transgressed the commandment of the Lord, and thy words because I feared the people, and obeyed their voice." And Saul spared the animals and some of the people of the land and brought the evil spirits into the land of the Israelites to dwell and spread there. And evil was let loose to plague and possess the souls of man until the day when Messiah came. And the spirits of the offspring of the Watchers possessed animal and people. It was a dark time when demons freely roamed the Earth.

But in the fullness of time it came to pass that Jesus came from Nazareth of Galilee, and was baptized by John in Jordan. And straightway coming up out of the water, he saw the heavens opened, and the Spirit like a dove descending upon him. And there came a voice from heaven, saying, "Thou art my beloved Son, in whom I am well pleased." And immediately the spirit driveth him into the wilderness.

Then was Jesus led up of the Spirit into the wilderness to be tempted of the devil. And when he had fasted forty days and forty nights, he was afterward hungered. And when the tempter came to him, he said, "If thou be the Son of God, command that these stones be made bread." But he answered and said, "It is written, 'Man shall not live by bread alone, but by every word that proceedeth out of the mouth of God.'"

Then the devil taketh him up into the holy city, and setteth him on a pinnacle of the temple, and saith unto him, "If thou be the Son of God, cast thyself down; for it is written, 'He shall give his angels charge concerning thee and in their hands they shall bear thee up, lest at any time thou dash thy foot against a stone.'"

Jesus said unto him, "It is written again, 'Thou shalt not tempt the Lord thy God.'"

Again, the devil taketh him up into an exceeding high mountain, and sheweth him all the kingdoms of the world, and the glory of them, and saith unto him, "All these things will I give thee, if thou wilt fall down and worship me."

Then saith Jesus unto him, "Get thee hence, Satan, for it is written, 'Thou shalt worship the Lord thy God, and him only shalt thou serve.'"

Then the devil leaveth him, and, behold, angels came and ministered unto him. For it is written, "Submit yourselves to God. Resist the devil, and he will flee from you."

Now when Jesus had heard that John was cast into prison, he departed into Galilee. Leaving Nazareth, he came and dwelt in Capernaum, which is upon the sea coast, in the borders of Zabulon and

Nephthalim; that it might be fulfilled which was spoken by Esaias the prophet, saying, "The land of Zabulon, and the land of Nephthalim, by the way of the sea, beyond Jordan, Galilee of the Gentiles, the people which sat in darkness saw great light; and to them which sat in the region and shadow of death light is sprung up."

And his fame went throughout all Syria and they brought unto him all sick people that were taken with diverse diseases and torments, and those who were possessed with devils, and those who were lunatic, and those that had the palsy; and he healed them. And there followed him great multitudes of people from Galilee, and from Decapolis, and from Jerusalem, and from Judea, and from beyond Jordan.

And Jesus came over unto the other side of the sea, into the country of the Gadarenes. And when he was come out of the ship, there were two possessed with devils, coming out of the tombs, exceeding fierce, so that no man might pass by that way. And, behold, they cried out, saying, "What have we to do with thee, Jesus, thou Son of God? Art thou come hither to torment us before the time?"

And one of the men came out of the tombs with an unclean spirit, who had his dwelling among the tombs; and no man could bind him, no, not with chains; because he had been often bound with fetters and chains, and the chains had been plucked asunder by him, and the fetters broken in pieces, neither could any man tame him. And always, night and day, he was in the mountains, and in the tombs, crying and cutting himself with stones.

But when he saw Jesus afar off, he ran and worshipped him, crying with a loud voice, and said, "What have I to do with thee, Jesus, thou Son of the most high God?"

"I adjure thee by God, that thou torment me not." For he said unto him, "Come out of the man, thou unclean spirit." And he asked him, "What is thy name?" And he answered, saying, "My name is Legion for we are many." And he besought him much that he would not send them away out of the country.

Now there was there nigh unto the mountains a great herd of swine feeding. And all the devils besought him, saying, "Send us into the swine, that we may enter into them."

And forthwith Jesus gave them leave. And the unclean spirits went out, and entered into the swine and the herd ran violently down a steep place into the sea, (they were about two thousand and were choked in the sea. And they that fed the swine fled, and told it in the city, and in the country. And they went out to see what it was that was done. And they came to Jesus, and saw him that was possessed with the devil, and had the legion, sitting, and clothed, and in his right mind: and they were afraid.

They that saw it told them how it befell him that was possessed with the devil and also concerning the swine. And they began to pray him to depart out of their coasts.

And when he was come into the ship, he that had been possessed with the devil prayed him that he might be with him. Howbeit Jesus suffered him not, but saith unto him, "Go home to thy friends, and tell them how great things the Lord hath done for thee, and hath had compassion on thee."

And he departed, and began to publish in Decapolis how great things Jesus had done for him and all men did marvel. And when Jesus was passed over again by ship unto the other side, much people gathered unto him and he was nigh unto the sea. And, behold, there cometh one of the rulers of the synagogue, Jairus by name; and when he saw him, he fell at his feet, And besought him greatly, saying, "My little daughter lieth at the point of death I pray thee, come and lay thy hands on her, that she may be healed and she shall live."

And Jesus went with him; and much people followed him, and thronged him.

And there was a certain woman, which had an issue of blood twelve years, and had suffered many things of many physicians, and had spent all that she had, and was nothing bettered, but rather grew worse. When she had heard of Jesus, she came in the press behind, and touched his garment. For she said, "If I may touch but his clothes, I shall be whole."

And straightway the fountain of her blood was dried up; and she felt in her body that she was healed of that plague. And Jesus, immediately knowing in himself that virtue had gone out of him, turned him about in the press, and said, "Who touched my clothes?"

And his disciples said unto him, "Thou seest the multitude thronging thee, and sayest thou, 'Who touched me?'" And he looked round about to see her that had done this thing. But the woman fearing and trembling, knowing what was done in her, came and fell down before him, and told him all the truth. And he said unto her, "Daughter, thy faith hath made thee whole; go in peace, and be whole of thy plague."

While he yet spake, there came from the ruler of the synagogue's house certain which said, "Thy daughter is dead, why troublest thou the Master any further?" As soon as Jesus heard the word that was spoken, he saith unto the ruler of the synagogue, "Be not afraid, only believe."

And having chosen twelve disciples, Jesus taught them and empowered them.

And as he sat upon the Mount of Olives, the disciples came unto him privately, saying, "Tell us, when shall these things be? And what shall be the sign of thy coming, and of the end of the world?"

And Jesus answered and said unto them, "Take heed that no man deceive you. For many shall come in my name, saying, 'I am Christ;' and shall deceive many. And ye shall hear of wars and rumors of wars, see that ye be not troubled for all these things must come to pass, but the end is not yet.

For nation shall rise against nation and kingdom against kingdom; and there shall be famines, and pestilences, and earthquakes, in diverse places. All these are the beginning of sorrows.

Then shall they deliver you up to be afflicted, and shall kill you and you shall be hated of all nations for my name's sake. And then shall many be offended, and shall betray one another, and shall hate one another.

And many false prophets shall rise, and shall deceive many. And because iniquity shall abound, the love of many shall wax cold. But he that shall endure unto the end, the same shall be saved.

And this gospel of the kingdom shall be preached in all the world for a witness unto all nations; and then shall the end come.

When you therefore shall see the abomination of desolation, spoken of by Daniel the prophet, stand in the holy place, whoso readeth, let him understand. Then let them which be in Judea flee into the mountains. Let him which is on the housetop not come down to take any thing out of his house. Neither let him which is in the field return back to take his clothes.

And woe unto them that are with child, and to them that give suck in those days! But pray ye that your flight be not in the winter, neither on the Sabbath day. For then shall be great tribulation, such as was not since the beginning of the world to this time, no, nor ever shall be.

And except those days should be shortened, there should no flesh be saved but for the elect's sake those days shall be shortened. Then if any man shall say unto you, 'Lo, here is Christ, or there;' believe it not. For there shall arise false Christs and false prophets, and shall shew great signs and wonders; insomuch that, if it were possible, they shall deceive the very elect.

Behold, I have told you before. Wherefore if they shall say unto you, 'Behold, he is in the desert;' go not forth. 'Behold, he is in the secret chambers;' believe it not. For as the lightning cometh out of the east, and shineth even unto the west; so shall also the coming of the Son of Man be. For wheresoever the carcass is, there will the eagles be gathered together."

Immediately after the tribulation of those days shall the sun be darkened, and the moon shall not give her light, and the stars shall fall from heaven, and the powers of the heavens shall be shaken. And then shall appear the sign of the Son of Man in heaven and then shall all the tribes of the earth mourn, and they shall see the Son of Man coming in the clouds of heaven with power and great glory.

And he shall send his angels with a great sound of a trumpet, and they shall gather together his elect from the four winds, from one end of heaven to the other. And while he had called unto him his twelve disciples, he gave them power against unclean spirits, to cast them out, and to heal all manner of sickness and all manner of disease.

Now the names of the twelve apostles are these: the first, Simon who is called Peter; Andrew his brother; James the son of Zebedee; and John his brother; Philip; Bartholomew; Thomas; Matthew the publican; James the son of Alphaeus; Lebbaeus, whose surname was Thaddaeus; Simon the Canaanite, and Judas Iscariot, who also betrayed him.

These twelve Jesus sent forth, and commanded them, saying, "Go not into the way of the Gentiles, and into any city of the Samaritans enter ye not. But go rather to the lost sheep of the house of Israel. And as ye go, preach, saying, 'The kingdom of heaven is at hand.' Heal the sick, cleanse the lepers, raise the dead, cast out devils; freely ye have received, freely give."

But the heart of Judas was greedy, for he was the treasurer and kept the money bag. And Judas wished to have Jesus establish his kingdom so that he could control the money for the nation. So he conceived a plan that would force Jesus to act or die. And from that time Judas sought opportunity to betray him.

Now the feast of unleavened bread drew nigh, which is called the Passover. And the chief priests and scribes sought how they might kill Jesus; for they feared the people.

Then entered Satan into Judas surnamed Iscariot, being of the number of the twelve. And he went his way, and communed with the chief priests and captains, how he might betray Jesus unto them. And they were glad, and covenanted to give him money.

And Judas said unto them, "What will ye give me, and I will deliver him unto you?" And they covenanted with him for thirty pieces of silver. And he promised, and sought opportunity to betray him unto them in the absence of the multitude.

Then came the day of unleavened bread, when the Passover must be killed. Now, on the first day of the feast of unleavened bread the disciples came to Jesus, saying unto him, "Where wilt thou that we prepare for thee to eat the Passover?"

And he said, "Go into the city to such a man, and say unto him, 'the Master saith, my time is at hand, I will keep the Passover at thy house with my disciples.'" And the disciples did as Jesus had appointed them; and they made ready the Passover.

Now when the even was come, he sat down with the twelve. And as they did eat, he said, "Verily I say unto you, that one of you shall betray me. The Son of Man goeth as it is written of him but woe unto that man by whom the Son of Man is betrayed! It had been good for that man if he had not been born."

And they were exceeding sorrowful, and began every one of them to say unto him, "Lord, is it I?" Jesus answered, "He it is, to whom I shall give a sop, when I have dipped it." And when he had dipped the sop, he gave it to Judas Iscariot, the son of Simon.

And after the sop Satan entered into him. Then said Jesus unto him, "That thou doest, do quickly."

Now no man at the table knew for what intent he spake this unto him. For some of them thought, because Judas had the bag, that Jesus had said unto him, "Buy those things that we have need of against the feast;" or, that he should give something to the poor.

Judas then having received the sop went immediately out and it was night.

Therefore, when he was gone out, Jesus said, "Now is the Son of Man glorified, and God is glorified in him. If God be glorified in him, God shall also glorify him in himself, and shall straightway glorify him.

"Little children, yet a little while I am with you. Ye shall seek me and as I said unto the Jews, 'Whither I go, ye cannot come;' so now I say to you.

"A new commandment I give unto you. That ye love one another as I have loved you. By this shall all men know that ye are my disciples, if ye have love one to another."

Simon Peter said unto him, "Lord, whither goest thou?" Jesus answered him, "Whither I go, thou canst not follow me now; but thou shalt follow me afterwards."

When Jesus had spoken these words, he went forth with his disciples over the brook Cedron where there was a garden, into which he entered, and his disciples.

And Judas also, who betrayed him, knew the place, for Jesus ofttimes resorted thither with his disciples. Judas then, having received a band of men and officers from the chief priests and Pharisees, cometh thither with lanterns and torches and weapons.

Jesus therefore, knowing all things that should come upon him, went forth, and said unto them, "Whom seek ye?" They answered him, "Jesus of Nazareth." Jesus saith unto them, "I am he."

And Judas also, which betrayed him, stood with them. As soon then as he had said unto them, I am he, they went backward, and fell to the ground. Then asked he them again, "Whom seek ye?" And they said, "Jesus of Nazareth." Jesus answered, "I have told you that I am he; if therefore ye seek me, let these go their way that the saying might be fulfilled, of which he spake. Of them which thou gavest me have I lost none."

When the morning was come, all the chief priests and elders of the people took counsel against Jesus to put him to death. And when they had bound him, they led him away, and delivered him to Pontius Pilate the governor.

Then Judas, who had betrayed him, when he saw that he was condemned, repented himself, and brought again the thirty pieces of silver to the chief priests and elders, saying, "I have sinned in that I have betrayed the innocent blood." And they said, "What is that to us? See thou to that."

And he cast down the pieces of silver in the temple, and departed, and went and hanged himself.

And the chief priests took the silver pieces, and said, "It is not lawful to put them into the treasury, because it is the price of blood." And they took counsel, and bought it with them to the potter's field. Wherefore that field was called the field of blood unto this day. Then was fulfilled that which was spoken by Jeremy the prophet, saying, "And they took the thirty pieces of silver, the price of him that was valued, whom they of the children of Israel did value; and gave them for the potter's field, as the Lord appointed me."

Then they took Jesus and beat him and laid a crown of thorns on his head and spit on him. And they crucified him, and parted his garments, casting lots that it might be fulfilled which was spoken by the prophet, "They parted my garments among them, and upon my vesture did they cast lots."

And set up over his head this accusation written, THIS IS JESUS THE KING OF THE JEWS. Then were there two thieves crucified with him, one on the right hand, and another on the left. And they that passed by reviled him, wagging their heads saying, "If thou be the Son of God, come down from the cross."

Likewise also the chief priests mocked him, with the scribes and elders, and said, "He saved others; himself he cannot save. If he be the King of Israel, let him now come down from the cross, and we will believe him."

"He trusted in God; let him deliver him now, if he will have him: for he said, 'I am the Son of God.'"

Now from the sixth hour there was darkness over all the land unto the ninth hour. And about the ninth hour Jesus cried with a loud voice, saying, "Eli, Eli, lama sabachthani?" That is to say, "My God, my God, why hast thou forsaken me?"

Some of them that stood there, when they heard that, said, "This man calleth for Elias." And straightway one of them ran, and took a sponge, and filled it with vinegar, and put it on a reed, and gave him to drink.

The rest said, "Let be, let us see whether Elias will come to save him." Jesus, when he had cried again with a loud voice, yielded up the ghost.

And, behold, the veil of the temple was rent in twain from the top to the bottom; and the earth did quake, and the rocks rent; and the graves were opened; and many bodies of the saints which slept arose.

Now when the centurion, and they that were with him, watching Jesus, saw the earthquake, and those things that were done, they feared greatly, saying, "Truly this was the Son of God."

The first day of the week cometh Mary Magdalene early, when it was yet dark, unto the sepulcher, and seeth the stone was taken away from the sepulcher. Then she runneth, and cometh to Simon Peter, and to the other disciple, whom Jesus loved, and saith unto them, "They have taken away the Lord out of the sepulcher, and we know not where they have laid him."

And returned from the sepulcher, and told all these things unto the eleven, and to all the rest. It was Mary Magdalene and Joanna, and Mary the mother of James, and other women that were with them, which told these things unto the apostles. And their words seemed to them as idle tales, and they believed them not.

So they ran both together and the other disciple did outrun Peter, and came first to the sepulcher.

And he stooping down, and looking in, saw the linen clothes lying; yet went he not in. Then cometh Simon Peter following him, and went into the sepulcher, and seeth the linen clothes lie, and the napkin, that was about his head, not lying with the linen clothes, but wrapped together in a place by itself.

Then went in also that other disciple, which came first to the sepulcher, and he saw, and believed. For as yet they knew not the scripture, that he must rise again from the dead. Then the disciples went away again unto their own home.

But Mary stood without at the sepulcher weeping and as she wept, she stooped down, and looked into the sepulcher, and seeth two angels in white sitting, the one at the head, and the other at the feet, where the body of Jesus had lain. And they say unto her, "Woman, why weepest thou?" She saith unto them, "Because they have taken away my Lord, and I know not where they have laid him." And when she had thus said, she turned herself back, and saw Jesus standing, and knew not that it was Jesus.

Jesus saith unto her, "Woman, why weepest thou? "Whom seekest thou?" She, supposing him to be the gardener, saith unto him, "Sir, if thou have borne him hence, tell me where thou hast laid him, and I will take him away."

Jesus saith unto her, "Mary." She turned herself, and saith unto him, "Rabboni," which is to say, Master. Jesus saith unto her, "Touch me not for I am not yet ascended to my Father but go to my brethren, and say unto them, 'I ascend unto my Father, and your Father and to my God, and your God.'"

Mary Magdalene came and told the disciples that she had seen the Lord, and that he had spoken these things unto her.

And, behold, Peter and another of them went that same day to a village called Emmaus, which was from Jerusalem about threescore furlongs. And they talked together of all these things which had happened. And it came to pass, that while they communed together and reasoned, Jesus himself drew near, and went with them. But their eyes were holden that they should not know him.

And he said unto them, "What manner of communications are these that ye have one to another, as ye walk, and are sad? And the one of them, whose name was Cleopas, answering said unto him, Art thou only a stranger in Jerusalem, and hast not known the things which are come to pass there in these days?

And he said unto them, "What things?" And they said unto him, "Concerning Jesus of Nazareth, which was a prophet mighty in deed and word before God and all the people. And how the chief priests and our rulers delivered him to be condemned to death, and have crucified him.

But we trusted that it had been he which should have redeemed Israel and beside all this, today is the third day since these things were done. Yea, and certain women also of our company made us astonished, which were early at the sepulcher. And when they found not his body, they came, saying, that they had also seen a vision of angels, which said that he was alive.

And certain of them which were with us went to the sepulcher, and found it even so as the women had said but him they saw not."

Then he said unto them, "O fools, and slow of heart to believe all that the prophets have spoken. Ought not Christ to have suffered these things, and to enter into his glory?"

And beginning at Moses and all the prophets, he expounded unto them in all the scriptures the things concerning himself. And they drew nigh unto the village, whither they went and he made as though he would have gone further. But they constrained him, saying, "Abide with us for it is toward evening, and the day is far spent." And he went in to tarry with them.

And it came to pass, as he sat at meat with them, he took bread, and blessed it, and brake, and gave to them.

Then the same day at evening, being the first day of the week, when the doors were shut where the disciples were assembled for fear of the Jews, came Jesus and stood in the midst, and saith unto them, "Peace be unto you."

And when he had so said, he shewed unto them his hands and his side. Then were the disciples glad, when they saw the Lord. And he said unto them, "Thus it is written, and thus it behooved Christ to suffer, and to rise from the dead the third day. And that repentance and remission of sins should be preached in his name among all nations, beginning at Jerusalem. And ye are witnesses of these things."

"And, behold, I send the promise of my Father upon you; but tarry ye in the city of Jerusalem, until ye be imbued with power from on high."

Then said Jesus to them again, "Peace be unto you; as my Father hath sent me, even so send I you." And when he had said this, he breathed on them, and saith unto them, "Receive ye the Holy Ghost." And their eyes were opened, and they knew him.

And he led them out as far as to Bethany, and he lifted up his hands, and blessed them. And it came to pass, while he blessed them, he was parted from them, and carried up into heaven.

Jesus Christ is the faithful witness, and the first begotten of the dead, and the prince of the kings of the earth. Unto him that loved us, and washed us from our sins in his own blood, And hath made us kings and priests unto God and his Father; to him be glory and dominion for ever and ever.

Behold, he cometh with clouds; and every eye shall see him, and they also which pierced him and all kindreds of the earth shall wail because of him.

"I am the Alpha and the Omega, the beginning and the ending," saith the Lord, "Which is and which was and which is to come; the Almighty. I am he that liveth and was dead; and, behold, I am alive for evermore, and have the keys of hell and of death."

And an angel came down from heaven, having the key of the bottomless pit and a great chain in his hand. And he laid hold on the dragon, that old serpent, which is the Devil, and Satan, and bound him a thousand years, And cast him into the bottomless pit, and shut him up, and set a seal upon him, that he should deceive the nations no more, till the thousand years should be fulfilled: and after that he must be loosed a little season.

And I saw thrones and they sat upon them, and judgment was

given unto them. And I saw the souls of them that were beheaded for the witness of Jesus, and for the word of God, and which had not worshipped the beast, neither his image, neither had received his mark upon their foreheads, or in their hands; and they lived and reigned with Christ a thousand years. But the rest of the dead lived not again until the thousand years were finished. This is the first resurrection.

Blessed and holy is he that hath part in the first resurrection, on such the second death hath no power, but they shall be priests of God and of Christ, and shall reign with him a thousand years.

And when the thousand years are expired, Satan shall be loosed out of his prison, and shall go out to deceive the nations which are in the four quarters of the earth, Gog, and Magog, to gather them together to battle, the number of whom is as the sand of the sea.

And they went up on the breadth of the earth, and compassed the camp of the saints about, and the beloved city. And those faithful to the Lord God were resolved to meet the force of darkness in battle. And their priests said to them, "Strengthen yourselves and do not fear them. Their craving for your death is formlessness and empty and their staff is as though it were not. Israel is all that is and shall be. It is in the eternal times to be. Today is God's appointed time to subdue and to abase the prince of wickedness. And God shall send eternal help to all of His redeemed by the might of an angel. He made the dominion of Michael magnificent in eternal light and has enlightened the covenant of Israel with happiness. Peace and blessing are in store for those who follow God.

We shall exalt Him among all the gods and the dominion of Michael and the rule of Israel will be exalted among all flesh. And righteousness shall be happy on high and all the sons of His truth shall rejoice in eternal knowledge. And you who are sons of His covenant, strengthen yourselves in the crucible of God until He waves His hand and fills His crucibles, His mysteries will be revealed to you according to your place and time.

You are the God of our covenant and we are your people, an eternal people, and you placed us in the source of light to see for your truth. And from the days of old you appointed a prince of light as our helper and all the spirits of truth are in his rule. It was you who (destined) made Belial for the pit, for he is an angel of enmity.

In darkness is his dominion. It is his way to make wicked and to make men guilty. And all the spirits of his kingdom are angels of violence. They walk in places of darkness and together their desire is for it. But we are the appointed of your truth. We shall rejoice in the hand of your might and we shall be glad in your salvation and we shall celebrate your help in our times of need. We desire your peace.

Who is like you in power, O God of Israel? Yet the poor you protect with your mighty hand. And which angel or prince is like the help of your might? For of old you appointed for yourself a day of battle to help with truth and to destroy guilt, to abase darkness, and to give might and light to your people. The sons of darkness are destined to an eternal place of annihilation. And happiness shall be the appointment of the sons of light."

Then their words were heard in the ears of God. And I looked, and behold a white cloud, and upon the cloud one sat like unto the Son of Man, having on his head a golden crown, and in his hand a sharp sickle. And another angel came out of the temple, crying with a loud voice to him that sat on the cloud, "Thrust in thy sickle, and reap for the time is come for thee to reap, for the harvest of the earth is ripe."

And he that sat on the cloud thrust in his sickle on the earth; and the earth was reaped. And another angel came out of the temple which is in heaven, he also having a sharp sickle. And another angel came out from the altar, which had power over fire and cried with a loud cry to him that had the sharp sickle, saying, "Thrust in thy sharp sickle, and gather the clusters of the vine of the earth; for her grapes are fully ripe."

And the angel thrust in his sickle into the earth, and gathered the vine of the earth, and cast it into the great winepress of the wrath of God. And the winepress was trodden without the city, and blood came out of the winepress, even unto the horse bridles, by the space of a thousand and six hundred furlongs.

And the devil that deceived them was cast into the lake of fire and brimstone, where the beast and the false prophet are, and shall be tormented day and night for ever and ever.

And I saw a great white throne, and him that sat on it, from whose face the earth and the heaven fled away; and there was found no place for them. And I saw the dead, small and great, stand before God; and the books were opened and another book was opened, which is the book of life, and the dead were judged out of those things which were written in the books, according to their works.

And the sea gave up the dead who were in it; and death and hell delivered up the dead who were in them: and they were judged every man according to their works.

And death and hell were cast into the lake of fire. This is the second death. And whosoever was not found written in the Book of Life was cast into the lake of fire.

And I saw a new heaven and a new earth; for the first heaven and the first earth were passed away. And there was no more sea. I saw the holy city, new Jerusalem, coming down from God out of heaven, prepared as a bride adorned for her husband. And I heard a great voice out of heaven saying, "Behold, the tabernacle of God is with men, and he will dwell with them, and they shall be his people, and God himself shall be with them, and be their God."

And God shall wipe away all tears from their eyes; and there shall be no more death, neither sorrow, nor crying, neither shall there be any more pain, for the former things are passed away.

And he that sat upon the throne said, "Behold, I make all things new." And he said unto me, "Write, for these words are true and faithful."

He said unto me, "It is done. I am the Alpha and the Omega, the beginning and the end. I will give unto him that is athirst of the fountain of the water of life freely."

"He that overcometh shall inherit all things and I will be his God, and he shall be my son."

The Omega

Evil walked the earth when angels fell. Evil stalks us now in disembodied spirits; immortal wraiths once clothed in flesh when angels and women bred; spirits released from their fleshly prisons when their bodies were destroyed for drinking the blood of men.

Evil also lives inside of the common man; set free when pride kills reason and devours integrity whole.

There is evil that entraps us and evil that tugs from within. But neither have control until we choose to relent. Evil is a choice of action, of thoughts entertained too long, of arrogance pushing aside the last vestiges of compassion.

Evil resides within the problem of choice. It is free will that convicts us. We are guilty of evil because we can choose to be holy. Free will is the very foundation of love, and the cornerstone of evil.

This problem of choice allows us to ascend to heaven or plummet to hell. We must choose…and to remain undecided is also a choice.

There is no way of knowing if the angels and demons wrapped in these pages are spirits of old or if they were travelers on a mission. It is impossible to know what mission these "gods" were attempting to accomplish. We may never know if the gods of Roman, Norse, and Greek myth were actually the men of renown mentioned in the Bible and if they were the Watchers or their offspring. What we do know is the church has killed those who held additional information or divergent views. We may never recover this lost information, but it is possible that the texts contained here may help us begin our search. (See Appendix "A" and "B")

About the Ancient Texts

The Dead Sea Scrolls found in the caves of Qumran are of great interest in the task of clarifying the history and doctrine in existence between biblical times and the fixing of canon. The scrolls were penned in the second century B.C. and were in use at least until the destruction of the second temple in 70 A.D. Similar scrolls to those found in the eleven caves of Qumran were also found at the Masada stronghold which fell to the Romans in 73 A.D.

Fragments of every book of the Old Testament except Esther were found in the caves of Qumran, as were many other ancient books. Some of these books are considered to have been of equal importance and influence to the people of Qumran and to the writers and scholars of the time. Writers of the New Testament were among those studying the scrolls found in Qumran. Knowing this, one might ask which of the dozens of non-canonical books most influenced the writers of the New Testament.

It is possible to ascertain the existence of certain influences within the Bible context by using the Bible itself. The Bible can direct us to other works in three ways. The work can be mentioned by name, as is the Book of Jasher. The work can be quoted within the Bible text, as is the case with the Book of Enoch. The existence of the work can be alluded to, as is the case of the missing letter from the apostle Paul to the Corinthians.

In the case of those books named in the Bible, one can compile a list. The list is lengthier than one might expect. Most of these works have not been found. Some have been unearthed but their authenticity is questioned. Others have been recovered and the link between scripture and scroll is generally accepted. Let us now take a look at the texts used to trace the history of evil.

The First Book of Adam and Eve: The Conflict With Satan

The First Book of Adam and Eve is an apocryphal story, written in a midrash style, detailing the life of Adam and Eve from the time God planted the Garden of Eden to the time that Cain killed his brother, Abel.

The story is an embellishment of the Genesis story up to the point of the cursing of Cain for the murder of Abel.

Of the numerous apocryphal works that were written regarding Adam and Eve this text seems to have most influenced early theologians. This is evident in the widespread popularity of the book from the third to the thirteenth century. Even though the book was widely read in the Middle Ages, and considered to shine light on what actually took place in the time of creation, today it is considered fiction and thus relegated to a collection of texts called the Pseudepigrapha, or "false writings."

The text shows some cobbling together of various works, combined into a single storyline. Although the foundation of the text can be traced to combined oral traditions thousands of years old, the primary story was likely created around two or three hundred years before Christ. Additions and details were added over many years, leading to this version being penned around the 3rd century A.D.

The text presented here is an embellishment of the Jewish storyline from Genesis that is "Christianized" by additions of allusions and references to the New Testament. Quite often the details of the story are made to foreshadow the birth, death, and resurrection of Jesus. The result is the text before you.

The central part of the text focuses on the conflict between Good and Evil in the form of Satan's endeavor to destroy God's creations, Adam and Eve. The story begs the eternal question, how does one know whether

God or Satan guides the opportunity, situation, or person confronting us. The fight between good and evil, as well as the question of who is influencing our surroundings, are eternal, and the story attempts to answer in metaphor.

The creation story and the tale of Adam and Eve pervaded the thoughts of writers throughout the ancient world. Evidence is seen in the large number of versions that exist in various languages and cultures. Indeed, it is due to the amazing popularity of the text that it has survived in six languages: Greek, Latin, Armenian, Georgian, and Slavonic, as well as a fragment in Coptic. The stories may also be traced through the writings of Greeks, Syrians, Egyptians, Abyssinians, Hebrews, and other ancient peoples.

Most scholars agree that the text was written originally in Greek and that all of the six versions show evidence of Greek linguistic roots. Those Greek manuscripts we have seem to be no more accurate to the original than any of the other translations, having been so many generations removed from the source document.

The foundation of our modern English translation began with the work of the Vicar of Broadwindsor, Dr. S. C. Malan, who worked from the Ethiopic edition, which was edited by, Professor at the University of Munich. Dr. Trumpp, who had the advantage of having an older version at his disposal.

From an ancient oral tradition, to a 3rd century codex, through the hands of Dr. E. Trumpp and Dr. S. C. Malan, to our modern English version, the First Book of Adam and Eve has survived, just as mankind has survived the struggles written of in the book itself.

The Malan translation of the text was penned in a rather stilted and formal style of English resembling that of the King James Bible. The Malan translation was then taken and re-written with word choices and sentence structure altered to make it more palatable and understandable to the modern reader, while keeping the poetic flow of the text.

The Second Book of Adam and Eve

The Second Book of Adam and Eve expands on the time from Cain's act of murder to the time Enoch was taken by God. It is, above all, a continuation of the story of The First Book of Adam and Eve.

Like the first book, this book is also part of the "Pseudepigrapha", which is a collection of historical biblical works that are considered to be fiction. Although considered to be Pseudepigrapha, it carries significance in that it provides insight into what was considered acceptable religious writing and ideas of the time.

This book is a composite of oral versions of an account handed down by word of mouth, from generation to generation until an unknown author pieced the stories together into a written form.

This particular version is the work of unknown Egyptians. The lack of historical allusion makes it difficult to date the writing. Using other Pseudepigrapha works as a reference only slightly narrows the probable dates to a range of a few hundred years. Parts of the text were probably included in an oral tradition, two or three hundred years before the birth of Christ. Certainly, book two was written after book one.

Sections of the text are found in the Jewish Talmud, and the Islamic Koran. Although some think this shows how the books of Adam and Eve played a vital role in ancient literature, it could just as well expose the fact that the authors of the Adam and Eve stories borrowed heavily from accepted holy books.

The Egyptian author wrote in Arabic, but later translations were found written in Ethiopic. The present English translation was completed in the late 1800's by Dr. S. C. Malan and Dr. E. Trumpp. They translated the text into King James English from both the Arabic version and the Ethiopic version, which was then published in The Forgotten Books of Eden in 1927 by The World Publishing Company. The version presented here takes the 1927 version, written in King James style English, and renders it into wording more familiar to the modern reader. Tangled sentence structure and archaic words were replaced with a clear, crisp, twenty-first century English.

The Book of Jasher

Jasher is not the author's name. Rather, it carries the meaning of something straight, true, or upright. The meaning could be the upright book or the faithful record, or it could refer to the character and reliability of the person(s) making the record.

The Bible references The Book of Jasher as a source of information and history in at least two places.

In the Book of Joshua is the account of an event that staggers the mind.

"And the sun stood still, and the moon stayed, until the people had avenged themselves upon their enemies. Is not this written in the book of Jasher? So the sun stood still in the midst of heaven, and hasted not to go down about a whole day." Joshua 10:13

One translation of a parallel chapter in the Book of Jasher states as follows:

"And when they were smiting, the day was declining toward evening, and Joshua said in the sight of all the people, Sun, stand thou still upon Gibeon, and thou moon in the valley of Ajalon, until the nation shall have revenged itself upon its enemies. And the Lord hearkened to the voice of Joshua, and the sun stood still in the midst of the heavens, and it stood still six and thirty moments, and the moon also stood still and hastened not to go down a whole day." Jasher 88:63-64

Another Biblical reference to Jasher shows David teaching archery to his army:

"Also he bade them teach the children of Judah the use of the bow; behold, it is written in the book of Jasher." 2 Samuel 1:18

The Jews of the first century A.D. held the Book of Jasher as a reliable historical document, although not "inspired." When Titus destroyed

Jerusalem in A.D. 70, one of his officers discovered a hidden library complete with a scholar hiding there. The officer had mercy on the man and took him and the books to his residence at Seville, Spain, (which was at that time the capital of the Roman province Hispalensis). The manuscript was later donated to the Jewish college at Cordova, Spain; and after printing was invented, the Jewish scholars had the book printed in Hebrew in Venice in 1625.

Confusion arose when another book of the same title was translated and released. This book, known now as Pseudo-Jasher, was discovered to be a hoax. Scholars turned against that book but continued to confuse it with the older document of the same name.

One of the printed manuscripts of Jasher from Spain was acquired by a British citizen named Samuel. Samuel set about to translate the book into English. When the British scholars heard of this, they made no distinction between the two books of Jasher and Pseudo-Jasher and the climate for publication turned stormy. Samuel sold his translation to Mordecai M. Noah, a New York publisher, who published it in 1840 as the first English translation. The copyright was later obtained by J. H. Parry and Company of Salt Lake City, Utah in 1887. It is a modern rendition of this version presented here.

The book seems to contain authentic Hebrew traditions and phraseology. Jasher, being a record, was added to and updated by each Hebrew historian as the book was handed down.

The book of Jasher we possess today was likely composed by an author compiling many old Jewish traditions (called Midrash) dating back to around the time of Christ. This included the source from the rescue of 70 A.D. Scholars agree that the Book of Jasher was likely last updated in Spain about the twelfth century A.D. It is difficult to know if Jasher is quoting

Midrash literature, or if Midrash literature was quoting the real Book of Jasher, which was also quoted in the Old Testament.

"Midrash" refers to writings containing extra-legal material of anecdotal or allegorical nature, designed either to clarify historical material, or to teach a moral point.

The names of the countries in which the sons of Noah are reported to have settled can definitely be dated to the eleventh century in Spain. This does not make it conclusive that the entire work must have been authored at that time. As books are copied, scribes can take it upon themselves to place the current names in the text.

Although Jasher was not considered inspired, it was considered to be a historical record reliable enough to be quoted by prophets and kings.

There are differences in authority and weight given to various types of records. Civil and historical records may serve the same historical purpose or record, but texts thought to be inspired have both historical and spiritual function.

When Ptolemy, King of Egypt, requested the Jewish holy books, the Israelites felt they could not give the Gentiles their sacred texts, so they sent him the Book of Jasher. He cherished it but later found it had a lesser status than the scriptures. Angry about the hoax, he confronted the Jews. Now with their heads at risk, they agreed to translate their Old Testament into Greek, which became known as the Septuagint.

The Lost Book of Enoch

(The Lost Book of Enoch and The Second Book of Enoch are printed in the single volume, The First and Second Books of Enoch: The Ethiopic and Slavonic Texts: A Comprehensive Translation with Commentary.")

Of all the books quoted, paraphrased, or referred to in the Bible, the Book of Enoch has influenced the writers of the Bible as few others have. The writers of the New Testament were frequently influenced by other writings, which set the theology and beliefs of the day. One of the main sources of theology regarding angels, demons, and the watchers was the Book of Enoch.

If a book is mentioned or quoted in the Bible is it not worthy of further study? The Book of Enoch was once cherished by Jews and Christians alike. It is still read today in certain Coptic Christian Churches in Ethiopia and is considered equal to all other books of the Bible.

Two versions of the Book of Enoch exist today. Most scholars date the Book of Enoch to sometime during the second century B.C. We do not know what earlier oral tradition, if any, the book contains. Enoch was considered inspired and authentic by certain Jewish sects of the first century B.C. and remained popular for at least five hundred years. The earliest Ethiopian text was apparently derived from a Greek manuscript of the Book of Enoch, which itself was a copy of an earlier text. The original was apparently written in the Semitic language, now thought to be Aramaic.

The Book of Enoch was discovered in the 18th century. It was thought that Enoch was penned after beginning of the Christian era. This theory was based upon the fact that it had quotes and paraphrases as well as concepts found in the New Testament. Thus, it was assumed that Enoch was heavily influenced by writers such as Jude and Peter.

However, recent discoveries of copies of the book among the Dead Sea Scrolls prove the book existed long before the time of Jesus Christ. These scrolls force a closer look and reconsideration. It becomes obvious that the New Testament did not influence the Book of Enoch; on the contrary, the Book of Enoch influenced the New Testament.

The date of the original writing upon which the second century B.C. Qumran copies were based is shrouded in obscurity. Likewise lost are the sources of the oral traditions that came to be the Book of Enoch.

It has been largely the opinion of historians that the book does not really contain the authentic words of the ancient prophet named Enoch, since he would have lived several thousand years earlier than the first known appearance of the book attributed to him. However, the first century Christians accepted the Book of Enoch as inspired, if not authentic.

They relied on it to understand the origin and purpose of many things, from angels to wind, sun, and stars. In fact, many of the key concepts used by Jesus Christ himself seem directly connected to terms and ideas in the Book of Enoch.

It is hard to avoid the evidence that Jesus not only studied the book, but also respected it highly enough to allude to its doctrine and content. Enoch is replete with mentions of the coming kingdom and other holy themes. It was not only Jesus who quoted phases or ideas from Enoch, there are over one hundred comments in the New Testament which find precedence in the Book of Enoch.

Other evidence of the early Christians' acceptance of the Book of Enoch was for many years buried under the King James Bible's mistranslation of Luke 9:35, describing the transfiguration of Christ: "And there came a voice out of the cloud, saying, 'This is my beloved Son. Hear him.'" Apparently, the translator wished to make this verse agree with a similar verse in Matthew and Mark. But Luke's verse in the original Greek reads: "This is my Son, the Elect One (from the Greek ho eklelegmenos, "the elect one"). Hear him."

The "Elect One" is a most significant term (found fourteen times) in the Book of Enoch. If the book was indeed known to the apostles of Christ, with its abundant descriptions of the Elect One who should "sit upon the throne of glory" and the Elect One who should "dwell in the midst of them," then the great scriptural authenticity is justly accorded to the Book of Enoch when the "voice out of the cloud" tells the apostles, "This is my Son, the Elect One." The one promised in the Book of Enoch.

The Book of Jude tells us in verse 14 that "Enoch, the seventh from Adam, prophesied." Jude, in verse 15, makes a direct reference to the Book of Enoch, where he writes, "to execute judgment on all, to convict all who are ungodly." As a matter of fact, it is a direct, word-for-word quote. Therefore, Jude's reference to the Enochian prophesies strongly leans toward the conclusion that these written prophecies were available to him at that time.

Fragments of ten Enoch manuscripts were found among the Dead Sea Scrolls. The number of scrolls indicates the Essenes (a Jewish commune or sect at the time of Christ) could well have used the Enochian writings as a community prayer book or teacher's manual and study text.

Many of the early church fathers also supported the Enochian writings. Justin Martyr ascribed all evil to demons he alleged to be the offspring of the angels who fell through lust for women; directly referencing the Enochian writings.

Athenagoras (170 A.D.) regarded Enoch as a true prophet. He describes the angels who "violated both their own nature and their office." In his writings, he goes into detail about the nature of fallen angels and the cause of their fall, which comes directly from the Enochian writings.

Since any book stands to be interpreted in many ways, Enoch posed problems for some theologians. Instead of reexamining their own theology, they sought to dispose of that which went counter to their beliefs. Some of the visions in Enoch are believed to point to the consummation of the age in conjunction with Christ's second coming which some believe took place in A.D. 70 (in the destruction of Jerusalem).

This being the case, it should not surprise us that Enoch was declared a fake and was rejected by Hilary, Jerome, and Augustine. Enoch was subsequently lost to Western Christendom for over a thousand years.

Enoch's "seventy generations" was also a great problem. Many scholars thought it could not be made to stretch beyond the First Century. Copies of Enoch soon disappeared. Indeed, for almost two thousand years we knew only the references made to it in the Bible. Without having the book itself, we could not have known it was being quoted in the Bible, sometimes word for word by Peter and Jude.

"...the Lord, having saved a people out of the land of Egypt, afterward destroyed them that believed not. And angels that kept not their own principality, but left their proper habitation, he hath kept in everlasting bonds under darkness unto the judgment of the great day. Even as Sodom and Gomorrah, and the cities about them...in like manner...are set out as examples...." Jude 5-7

"For if God spared not the angels when they sinned, but cast them down into hell, and committed them to pits of darkness, to be reserved unto judgment," 2 Peter 2-4.

To what extent other New Testament writers regarded Enoch as scriptural canon may be determined by comparing their writings with those found in Enoch. A strong possibility of influence upon their thought and choice of wording is evidenced by a great many references found in Enoch which remind one of passages found in the New Testament.

The Book of Enoch seems to be a missing link between Jewish and Christian theology and is considered by many to be more Christian in its theology than Jewish. It was considered scripture by many early Christians. The literature of the church fathers is filled with references to this book. The early second century apocryphal book of the Epistle of Barnabas makes many references and quotes from the Book of Enoch. Second and third century church fathers like Justin Martyr, Irenaeus, Origin and Clement of Alexandria all seemed to have accepted Enoch as authentic. Tertullian (160-230 A.D.) even called the Book of Enoch, "Holy Scripture."

The Ethiopian Coptic Church holds the Book of Enoch as part of its official spiritual canon. It was widely known and read the first three centuries after Christ. This and many other books became discredited after the Council of Laodicea. And being under ban of the authorities, it gradually disappeared from circulation.

In 1773, rumors of a surviving copy of the book drew Scottish explorer James Bruce to distant Ethiopia. He found the Book of Enoch had been preserved by the Ethiopian church, which put it right alongside the other books of the Bible.

Bruce secured not one, but three Ethiopian copies of the book and brought them back to Europe and Britain. In 1773 Bruce returned from six years in Abyssinia. In 1821 Richard Laurence published the first English translation. The famous R.H. Charles edition was published in 1912. In the following years several portions of the Greek text surfaced. Then with the discovery of cave 4 at Qumran, seven fragmentary copies of the Aramaic text were discovered.

Even in its complete form, the Book of Enoch is not one manuscript. It is a composite of several manuscripts written by several authors. Enoch and Noah each have pieces of the book ascribed to them. Yet still today the most complete text of the multifaceted book is the Ethiopian copy.

Later, another "Book of Enoch" surfaced. This text, dubbed "2 Enoch" and commonly called "the Slavonic Enoch," was discovered in 1886 by Professor Sokolov in the archives of the Belgrade Public Library. It appears that just as the Ethiopian Enoch ("1 Enoch") escaped the sixth-century Church suppression of Enoch texts in the Mediterranean area, so a Slavonic Enoch survived far away, long after the originals from which it was copied were destroyed or hidden.

Specialists in the Enochian texts believe that the missing original from which the Slavonic was copied was probably a Greek manuscript, which itself may have been based on a Hebrew or Aramaic manuscript.

The Slavonic text is evidence of many later additions to the original manuscript. Unfortunately, later additions and the deletion of teachings considered erroneous, rendered the text unreliable.

Because of certain references to dates and data regarding certain calendar systems in the Slavonic Enoch, some claim the text cannot be earlier than the seventh century A.D. Some see these passages not as evidence of Christian authorship, but as later Christian interpolations into an earlier manuscript. Enochian specialist R.H. Charles, for instance, believes that even the better of the two Slavonic manuscripts contains interpolations and is, in textual terms, "corrupt." It is for the reasons above, we will look only at the book referred to as 1 Enoch. We will leave the inferior manuscript of 2 Enoch for another day.

The translations used for this work are taken from both the Richard Laurence and R.H. Charles manuscripts in addition to numerous sources and commentaries. The texts were compared and, in some cases, transliterated for easier reading by the modern "American" English reader as some phrasing from the 18th and 19th centuries may seem somewhat clumsy to our 21st century eyes.

The Second Book of Enoch: Slavonic Enoch

As part of the Enochian literature, The Second Book of Enoch is included in the pseudepigraphal corpus.

Pseudepigrapha : Spurious or pseudonymous writings, especially Jewish writings ascribed to various biblical patriarchs and prophets but composed within approximately 200 years of the birth of Jesus Christ.

In 1773, rumors of a surviving copy of an ancient book drew Scottish explorer James Bruce to distant Ethiopia. There, he found the "First Book of Enoch." Later, another "Book of Enoch" surfaced. The text, which is known as "Second Enoch," was discovered in 1886 by Professor Sokolov in the archives of the Belgrade Public Library. The Second Book of Enoch was written in the latter half of the first century A.D. The text was preserved only in Slavonic and consequently bears the designation, "Slavonic Enoch." The text has also been known by the titles of "2 Enoch", and "The Secrets of Enoch." 2 Enoch is basically an expansion of Genesis 5:21-32, taking the reader from the time of Enoch to the onset of the great flood of Noah's day.

The main theme of the book is the ascension of Enoch progressively through multiple heavens. During the ascension Enoch is transfigured into an angel and granted access to the secrets of creation. Enoch is then given a 30 day grace period to return to earth and instruct his sons and all the members of his household regarding everything God had revealed to him. The text reports that after period of grace an angel will then come to retrieve him to take him from the earth.

Many credible versions end with chapter 68, however there is a longer version of 2 Enoch, which we will examine. In this version the wisdom and insights given to the family of Enoch is passed from family members to Melchizedek, whom God raises up as an archpriest. Melchizedek then fulfills the function of a prophet-priest. To pave the way to Melchizedek, Methuselah functions as a priest for ten years and then passed his station on to Nir, Noah's younger brother. Nir's wife, Sopanim, miraculously conceives without human intercourse while about to die and posthumously gives birth to Melchizedek, who is born with the appearance and maturity of a three-year old child and the symbol of the priesthood on his chest.

The world is doomed to suffer the flood but Michael the archangel promises Melchizedek salvation. This establishes his priesthood for all of eternity. The text goes on to report that in the last generation, there will be another Melchizedek who will be "the head of all, a great archpriest, the Word and Power of God, who will perform miracles, greater and more glorious than all the previous ones".

The manuscripts, which contain and preserve this document, exist only in Old Slavonic. Of the twenty or more manuscripts dating from the 13th century A.D. no single one contains the complete text of 2 Enoch. When pieced together there appears to be two versions. These we will refer to as the long and short version.

The difference in length between the two is due to two quite different features. There are blocks of text found only in the longer manuscripts; but even when the passages are parallel, the longer manuscripts tend to be more full and detailed. At the same time there is so much verbal similarity when the passages correspond that a common source must be supposed.

The form of 2 Enoch is what one finds in Jewish Wisdom literature and
Jewish Apocalyptic literature. It has been suggested that the longer version
is characterized by editorial expansions and Christian interpolations. Hence,
the shorter version contains fewer Christian elements. The author of 2
Enoch speaks much of the Creator and final judgment, but he speaks very
little, about redemption, which seems to be absent from the thoughts of the
author. Indeed, there seems to be a total lack of a Savior or Redeemer in 2
Enoch. What is noteworthy is that 2 Enoch has no reference to the mercy of
God.

In the long version presented here, it appears that the last portion of the text
was added as an afterthought. It contains the rise of Melchizedek. The
appearance of Melchizedek ties 2 Enoch to several other texts forming a
Melchizedkian tradition. The author of 2 Enoch follows a tradition in which
an aged mother, who had been barren up to her deathbed, miraculously
conceived Melchizedek without human intervention. Before she was able to
give birth to the baby she died. The baby then emerged from her dead body
with the maturity of a three-year-old boy. His priesthood will be
perpetuated throughout the generations until "another Melchizedek"
appears. If the last Melchizedek serves as the archpriest for the last
generation, it indicates that in the mind of this Jewish writer, the Temple
was to be rebuilt and would be the place were God would meet His people
when the heathen nations were destroyed. The continuation and victory of
the Jews as the selected and blessed people of God is implied. In this vein, 2
Enoch follows certain apocalyptic writings.

   (For more information on apocalyptic writings see "End of Days" by
Joseph Lumpkin.)

The Slavonic version is translated from a Greek source. Most scholars agree that there was either a Hebrew or Aramaic original lying behind the Greek source from which the Slavonic manuscripts were produced. The Hebrew origins are indicated by "Semitisms" in the work, but there are also Greek words and expressions, such as the names of the planets in chapter 30.

Proof that The Slavonic Enoch was written in Greek is shown by the derivation of Adam's name, and by several coincidences with the Septuagint. The origin of the story is perhaps based on Hebrew traditions and certain Semitic turns of language show up in the text. This tends to indicate that there was at one time a Hebrew or Aramaic text that preceded the Greek. From the Greek it was translated into Slavonic. Of this version there are five manuscripts or pieces thereof found.

 The short version or the Slavonic Enoch was probably written by a single author in an attempt to bring all the current traditions about Enoch of his time into a central storyline and system. The schema to accomplish the unity of traditions implements Enoch's ascension through multiple heavens. This author was probably a Jew living in Egypt. There are several elements in the book, which betray Egyptian origin. The longer version of 2 Enoch was seeded with Christian elements and appended with an ending that does not fit well, illuminating the fact that there were several authors involved in the longer version.

Parts of the book were probably written in the late first century A.D. The first date is a limit set by the fact that Ethiopic Enoch, Ecclesiasticus, and Wisdom of Solomon are used as sources or references within the text; the second date is a limit set by the fact that the destruction of the Temple is not mentioned at all.

The Slavonic Enoch furnishes new material for the study of religious thought in the beginning of the Common Era. The ideas of the millennium and of multiple heavens are the most important in this connection. Another very interesting feature is the presence of evil in heaven, the fallen angels in the second heaven, and hell in the third. The idea of evil in heaven may be a nod to the book of Job and the dialog between God and Satan, who was coming and going between heaven and earth. The idea of hell in the third heaven may have been derived from ideas expressed in the Old Testament book of Isaiah, which mentions that the sufferings of the wicked will be witnessed by the righteous in paradise.

Chapter 21 and forward for several chapters shows a heavy influence of Greek mythology. The Zodiac is mentioned along with heavenly bodies with names such as Zeus, Cronus, Aphrodite, and others. The part of the text containing names and astrological descriptions could have been tampered with as late as the seventh century A.D.

By far, the most interesting and confusing section begins around chapter 25 and runs for several chapters. Here the text takes a turn toward Gnostic theology and cosmology. The Gnostics were a Christian sect, which formed and grew in the first century A.D. and thrived in the second century A.D.

Although Gnostic borrowed from Plato's (428 B.C. – 348 B.C.) creation myth, the maturity and construction of the story shows it to be of Gnostic Christian origin, placing it no earlier than the last part of the first century A.D. and no later than the end of the Second century. Add to the dating question the fact that the destruction of the Temple in Jerusalem is not mentioned, which leads to a date just before 70 A.D., if one assumes the Gnostic flavor was not added later.

The history of the text is obviously long and varied. It probably began as a Jewish oral tradition with pieces taken from several Enochian stories. It was first penned in Hebrew or Aramaic. The date of this incarnation of the text is unknown. Later, the story was expanded and embellished by Greek influences. Lastly, Christians and Gnostics commandeered the book and added their own matter. Thus 2 Enoch exhibits a kaleidoscope of cultural and religious contributions over a great scope of time from the first century B.C. (assuming it came after 1 Enoch) and ending as late as the seventh century A.D. These additions would allow any serious student insight into how ancient texts evolve.

Second Enoch was rediscovered and published in the early 19th century A.D. The text uses the R. H. Charles and W. R. Morfill translation of 1896 with additions from other sources. Archaic terms and sentence structure were revised or explained to convey a more modern rendering for the twenty-first century readers.

The Book of Jubilees

The Book of Jubilees, also known as The Little Genesis and The Apocalypse of Moses, opens with an extraordinary claim of authorship. It is attributed to the very hand of Moses; penned while he was on Mount Sinai, as an angel of God dictated to him regarding those events that transpired from the beginning of the world. The story is written from the viewpoint of the angel.

The angelic monolog takes place after the exodus of the children of Israel out of Egypt. The setting is atop Mount Sinai, where Moses was summoned by God. The text then unfolds as the angel reveals heaven's viewpoint of history. We are led through the creation of man, Adam's fall from grace, the union of fallen angels and earthly women, the birth of demonic offspring, the cleansing of the earth by flood, and the astonishing claim that man's very nature was somehow changed, bringing about a man with less sinful qualities than his antediluvian counterpart.

The story goes on to fill in many details in Israel's history, ending at the point in time when the narrative itself takes place, after the exodus.

Scholars believe Jubilees was composed in the second century B.C. The Hebrew fragments found at Qumran are part of a Jewish library that contained other supporting literature such as the Book of Enoch and others.

An analysis of the chronological development in the shapes of letters in the manuscripts confirms that Jubilees is pre-Christian in date and seems to have been penned between 100 and 200 B.C. The book of Jubilees is also cited in the Qumran Damascus Document in pre-Christian texts.

The author was a Pharisee (a doctor of the law), or someone very familiar with scripture and religious law. Since the scrolls were found in what is assumed to be an Essene library, and were dated to the time the

Essene community was active, the author was probably a member of that particular religious group. Jubilees represents a hyper-legalistic and midrashic tendency, which was part of the Essene culture at the time.

Jubilees represents a midrash on Genesis 1:1 through Exodus 12 depicting the episodes from creation with the observance of the Sabbath by the angels and men; to Israel's escape from Egyptian bondage.

Although originally written in Hebrew, the Hebrew texts were completely lost until the find at Qumran. Fragments of Jubilees were discovered among the Dead Sea Scrolls. At least fourteen copies of the Book of Jubilees have been identified from caves 1, 2, 3 and 11 at Qumran. This makes it clear that the Book of Jubilees was a popular and probably authoritative text for the community whose library was concealed in the caves. These fragments are actually generations closer to the original copies than most books in our accepted Bible. Unfortunately, the fragments found at Qumran were only pieces of the texts and offered the briefest of glimpses of the entire book. The only complete versions of the Book of Jubilees are in Ethiopic, which in turn were translations of a Greek version.

Four Ethiopian manuscripts of Jubilees were found to be hundreds of years old. Of these, the fifteenth and sixteenth century texts are the truest and least corrupted when compared to the fragments found at Qumran. There are also citations of Jubilees in Syriac literature that may reflect a lost translation from Hebrew. Pieces of Latin translations have also been found.

Other fragments of a Greek version are quoted or referenced by Justin Martyr, Origen, Diodorus of Antioch, Isidore of Alexandria, Isidore of Seville, Eutychius, Patriarch of Alexandria, John of Malala, and Syncellus. This amount of varied information and translations is enough to allow us to reconstruct the original to a great degree. The internal evidence of Jubilees shows very little tampering by Christians during its subsequent translations, allowing a clear view of certain Jewish beliefs propagated at the time of its origin. By removing certain variances, we can isolate

Christian alterations and mistakes in translations with a reasonable degree of confidence. Due to the poor condition of the fragments of Qumran, we may never be able to confirm certain key phrases in Hebrew. Thus, as with many texts, including the Bible, in the end we must trust in the accuracy of the ancient translators.

It should be noted that the books of Jubilees, Enoch, and Jasher present stories of "The Watchers," a group of angels sent to earth to record and teach, but who fell by their own lust and pride into a demonic state. Both Enoch and Jubilees refer to a solar-based calendar. This may show a conflict or transition at the time of their penning since Judaism now uses a lunar-based calendar.

Laws, rites, and functions are observed and noted in Jubilees. Circumcision is emphasized in both humans and angels. Angelic observance of Sabbath laws as well as parts of Jewish religious laws are said to have been observed in heaven before they were revealed to Moses.

To the Qumran community, complete obedience to the Laws of Moses entailed observing a series of holy days and festivals at a particular time according to a specific calendar. The calendar described in Jubilees is one of 364 days, divided into four seasons of three months each with thirteen weeks to a season. Each month had 30 days with one day added at certain times for each of the four seasons. With 52 weeks in a year, the festival and holy days recur at the same point each year. This calendar became a hallmark of an orthodox Qumran community.

The adherence to a specific calendar is one of many ways the Book of Jubilees shows the devotion to religious law. The law had been placed at the pinnacle of importance in the lives of the community at Qumran. All aspects of life were driven by a seemingly obsessive compliance to every jot and tittle of the law. The Book Of Jubilees confirms what can only be inferred from the books of Ezra, Nehemiah, and Zechariah, that the law and those who carried it out were supreme.

As the law took hold, by its nature, it crystallized the society. Free expression died, smothered under a mantle of hyper-orthodoxy. Since free thought invited accusations of violations of the law or claims of heresy, prudence, a closed mind, and a silent voice prevailed. Free thought was limited to religious or apocryphal writings, which upheld the orthodox positions of the day. The silent period between Malachi and Mark may be a reflection of this stasis. Jubilees, Enoch, and other apocryphal books found in the Qumran caves are a triumph over the unimaginative mindset brought on by making religious law supreme and human expression contrary to the law and punishable by death. It may be an odd manifestation that such a burst of creativity was fueled by the very search for order that suppressed free thought in the first place.

The Book of Jubilees seems to be an attempt to answer and explain all questions left unanswered in the Book of Genesis as well as to bolster the position of the religious law. It attempts to trace the source of religious laws back to an ancient beginning thereby adding weight and sanction.

In the Book of Jubilees, we discover the origin of the wife of Cain. There is information offered about angels and the beginnings of the human race, how demons came into existence, and the place of Satan in the plans of God. Information is offered in an attempt to make perfect sense of the vagaries left in Genesis. For the defense of order and law and to maintain religious law as the center point of Jewish life, Jubilees was written as an answer to both pagan Greeks and liberal Jews. From the divine placement of law and order to its explanation of times and events, Jubilees is a panorama of legalism.

The name "Jubilees" comes from the division of time into eras known as Jubilees. One Jubilee occurs after the equivalent of forty-nine years, or seven Sabbaths of weeks of years have passed. It is the numerical perfection of seven sevens. In a balance and symmetry of years, the Jubilee occurs after seven cycles of seven or forty-nine years have been completed. Thus, the fiftieth year is a Jubilee year. Time is told by referencing the number of Jubilees that have transpired from the time the festival was first kept. For example, Israel entered Canaan at the close of the fiftieth jubilee, which is about 2450 B.C.

The obsession with time, dates, and the strict observance of festivals are all evidence of legalism taken to the highest level.

Based on the approximate time of writing, Jubilees was created in the time of the Maccabees, in the high priesthood of Hyrcanus. In this period of time the appearance of the Messiah and the rise of the Messianic kingdom were viewed as imminent. Followers were preparing themselves for the arrival of the Messiah and the establishment of His eternal kingdom.

Judaism was in contact with the Greek culture at the time. The Greeks were known to be philosophers and were developing processes of critical thinking. One objective of Jubilees was to defend Judaism against the attacks of the Hellenists and to prove that the law was logical, consistent, and valid. Attacks against paganism and non-believers are embedded in the text along with defense of the law and its consistency through proclamations of the law being observed by the angels in heaven from the beginning of creation.

Moral lessons are taught by use of the juxtaposition of the "satans" and their attempts to test and lead mankind into sin against the warning and advice of scriptural wisdom from Moses and his angels.

Mastema is mentioned only in The Book of Jubilees and in the Fragments of a Zadokite Work. Mastema is Satan. The name Mastema is derived from the Hebrew, "Mastim," meaning "adversary." The word occurs as singular and plural. The word is equivalent to Satan (adversary or accuser). This is similar to the chief Satan and his class of "satans" in 1 Enoch 40,7.

Mastema is subservient to God. His task is to tempt men to sin and if they do, he accuses them in the presence of the Throne of God. He and his minions lead men into sin but do not cause the sin. Once men have chosen to sin, they lead them from sin to destruction. Since man is given free will, sin is a choice, with Mastema simply encouraging and facilitating the decision. The choice, we can assume, is our own and the destruction that follows is "self-destruction."

Beliar is also mentioned. Beliar is the Greek name for Belial / Beliaal. The name in its Hebrew equivalent means "without value." This was a demon known by the Jews as the chief of all the devils. Belial is the leader of the Sons of Darkness. Belial and Mastema are mentioned in a Zadokite fragment saying that at the time of the Antichrist, Belial shall be let loose against Israel; as God spoke through Isaiah the prophet. Belial is sometimes presented as an agent of God's punishment although he is considered a "Satan."

It is important to mention that Judaism had no doctrine of original sin. The fall of Adam and Eve may have removed man from the perfect environment and the curses that followed may have shortened his lifespan, but propagation of sin through the bloodline was not considered. In the book of Jubilees, sin seemed to affect only man and the animals he was given dominion over. Yet man continued to sin, and to increase in his capacity and modes of sin. The explanation offered for man's inability to resist is the existence of fallen angels; spiritual, superhuman creatures whose task it was to teach us but who now tempted and misled men. In the end, the world declines and crumbles under the evil influence of the fallen angels turned demons called, "The Watchers."

With the establishment of the covenant between Abraham and God, we are told that God had appointed spirits to "mislead" all the nations but would not assign a spirit to lead or mislead the children of Isaac as God himself would be leading them.

The angels converse in Hebrew as it is the heavenly tongue. The law is written by God using this alphabet thus the law is also holy. All men spoke Hebrew until the time of Babel when the Hebrew language was lost. However, when Abraham dedicated himself to God, his ears were opened and his tongue was sanctified and Hebrew was again spoken and understood.

Finally, the entire text is based on the numbers of forty-nine and fifty. Forty-nine represents the pinnacle of perfection, being made up of seven times seven. The number fifty, which is the number of the Jubilee, is the number of grace. In the year of Jubilee slaves were to be set free, debts were forgiven, and grace filled the land and people.

Drawing from the theology and myths at the time, the Book of Jubilees expands and embellishes on the creation story, the fall of Adam and Eve, and the fall of the angels. The expanded detail written into the text may have been one reason it was eventually rejected. However, the effects of the book can still be seen throughout the Judeo-Christian beliefs of today. The theology espoused in Jubilees can be seen in the angelology and demonology taught in the Christian churches of today and widely held by many Jews.

In an attempt to answer questions left unaddressed in Genesis the writer confronts the origin and identification of Cain's wife. According to the Book Of Jubilees, Cain married his sister, as did all of the sons of Adam and Eve, except Abel, who was murdered. This seemed offensive to some, since it flies in the face of the very law it was written to defend. Yet this seemed to the writer to be the lesser of evils, given the problematic questions. Inbreeding was dismissed with the observation that the law was not fully given and understood then. The effects of the act were moot due to the purity of the newly created race.

The seeming discrepancy between the divine command of Adam's death decree and the timing of his death is addressed. Seeing that Adam continued to live even after he ate the fruit, which was supposed to bring on his death, the writer set about to clarify God's actions. The problem is explained away is a single sentence. Since a day in heaven is as a thousand years on earth and Adam died having lived less than a thousand years this meant he died in the same heavenly day. Dying within the same day of the crime was acceptable.

In an astonishing parallel to the Book of Enoch, written at about the same time as Jubilees, the Watchers, or sons of God mentioned in Genesis 6, fell from grace when they descended to earth and had sex with the daughters of men. In the Book of Enoch, the angels descended for the purpose of seducing the women of earth.

However, in The Book of Jubilees, the angels were sent to teach men, but after living on earth for a while, they were tempted by their own lust and fell from heaven. The offspring of this unholy union were bloodthirsty and cannibalistic giants.

The Book of Jubilees indicates that each of the offspring was somehow different. Because of this, they are divided into categories of the Nephilim (or Naphidim, depending on the transliteration), the Giants, and the Eljo. The Nephil are mentioned however this word is the singular of Nephilim. Therefore, we have these classifications or species living on the earth: Angels, also referred to as watchers; Nephilim; Eljo; Giants; and Human.

The Nephilim seem to be a being that contains an evil spirit much like their fathers. The giants, although coming from the same union of angel and woman, were carnal creatures. We have little information about the Eljo except they lived to kill men. They could be the "men of renown" mentioned in the Bible. These may have been the beings that brought about the myths of the violent and angry creatures such as the Cyclops or gods of war.

As sin spread throughout the world and the minds of men were turned toward evil, God saw no alternative but to cleanse the earth with a flood and establish a "new nature" in man that does not have to sin. It is this new nature that the Messiah will meet in mankind when He comes. As far as this author is aware, the re-creation of man's nature is mentioned in no other book. This idea of human nature being altered as it existed before the flood is found nowhere else but in Jubilees.

The angelic narrator tells us there were times in Israel's history when no evil existed and all men lived in accord. We are also told when and where the satans were allowed to attack and confound Israel. In this narrative, God uses his satans to harden the hearts of the Egyptians so they pursued Israel and were destroyed.

"The Apocalypse of Moses" also denotes the same work. This title seems to have been used for only a short period of time. It refers to the revelation given to Moses as the recipient of all the knowledge disclosed in the book. The term "Apocalypse" means to make known or to reveal. Another title of Jubilees is "Little Genesis". This refers to the lesser, non-canon status of the book. With the exception of minor differences picked up through translation and copying, the three titles represent the same text.

The War Scroll

In 1955, the War Scroll was found in Cave 1 at Qumran. Other fragments were found in Cave 4. The 19 columns of the scroll were badly mutilated. After great pains, the fragments were deciphered and published by the Hebrew University in Jerusalem

The War Scroll is thought to have been written sometime after the mid-first century BCE to the beginning of the 1st Century CE. The author of the manuscript made use of the Book of Daniel. The War Scroll contains rules for the military, religious preparations, and how the fighting was to be conducted.

In the War Scroll we see the sons of light, who are the remnants of the Jewish faithful, exiled into the wilderness by an ever-darkening world. Out of the wilderness of Jerusalem they return to fight against the sons of darkness, the children of Belial, in the last days. This fits in very well with our accepted prophecies in the book of Revelation.

The Book of Genesis

Genesis is the first book of the Old Testament in both the Jewish and Christian Bibles. Genesis means the act or process of producing, thus the text is named for the creation story.

The first eleven chapters are adapted from Mesopotamian and Canaanite traditions regarding the creation of earth. Other story lines were added to account for the existence of man by incorporating stories about Adam and Eve. The story of the flood is brought into Genesis, although it is difficult to know exactly which region the story was taken from as practically every culture has such a story. It is generally assumed the Deluge story was acquired from the same culture which the creation story element was taken.

Although traditionally The Book of Genesis is attributed to Moses, most modern scholars agree that the book is a composite of at least three different literary strands: J (10th century B.C.), E (9th century), and P (5th century). Oddly, one of the contributors seems to have a "feminine" voice and could have been penned, or at least influenced by a woman.

At the time of the "J" document, a despot ruled over the Jews around 560 B.C. The writer of "J" may have written the book to document the people's oral history and thus give them hope and ensure there would be a record of their connection to their God, fearing their destruction.

Since three stories were being interwoven, the writer of Genesis took the J,P, and E stories and combined them, removing parts that were contrary to the religious beliefs of the day. One set of writings used the Canaanite term, "Elohim," as the name of the creator God. A second used the more ancient Judean word transliterated from Hebrew and rendered "Jehovah" in English, to describe its God.

By removing inconsistencies and repetitions a smooth storyline emerged. The story coming from the Canaanite culture contained polytheistic beliefs. Traces of the two different gods and their differing personalities, as well as the Canaanite belief in polytheism may remain, but since the Jews had come to embrace monotheism at that time, the writer attempted to remove traces of such variances.

For a more complete picture it is always best to keep all stories and books in context. The complete translations of the non-biblical books used in this work can be obtained in "The Lost Books of the Bible: The Great Rejected Texts" by Joseph Lumpkin, published by Fifth Estate.

The Lost Books of the Bible: The Great Rejected Texts

The Lost Books of the Bible: The Great Rejected Texts -
Eighteen of the most sought after books available, which shed light on the
evolution of our faith, our theology, and our church. Translations and
commentary by the author of the best selling book, "The Lost Book of
Enoch," Joseph B. Lumpkin.
- Section One: Lost Scriptures of the Old Testament- First Book of Adam and
Eve, Second Book of Adam and Eve, First Book of Enoch, Second Book of
Enoch (Secrets of Enoch), Jubilees, Jasher, The Story of Ahikar
- Section Two: Apocalyptic Writings and the End of Days- Apocalypse of
Abraham, Apocalypse of Thomas 4 Ezra, 2 Baruch, War Scroll (Sons of Dark
vs. Sons of Light)
- Section Three: Lost Scriptures of the New Testament- Gospel of Philip,
Gospel of Mary Magdalene, Apocryphon of John, Gospel of Thomas, Gospel
of Judas, Acts Chapter 29

Appendix "A"

Egyptian Gods and Goddesses

Aken - Ferryman of the Underworld
Aker - Guardian to the Underworld
Ammit - Devourer of the Wicked
Amun Re - The King of the Gods
Anat - Mother of Gods
Anqet - Goddess of Fertility
Anubis - God of Embalming
Anuke - Goddess of War
Apep - The Great Destroyer
Aten - The Sun Disk and later God
Atum - The All-Father
Baal - God of Thunder
Bast - Cat-Goddess
Bat - Cow Goddess
Benu (Bennu) - The Bird of Creation
Bes - Protector of Childbirth
Denwen - The Serpent
Geb - God of the Earth
Hathor - Goddess of Music and Dance
Heryshef - Ruler of the Riverbanks
Heset - Goddess of Plenty
Hike - God of Magic and Medicine
Horus - King of the Gods on Earth
Hu - God of the Spoken Word
Imhotep - God of Science and Reason
Isis - Queen of the Gods
Iusaas - Creator Goddess
Kek - God of Darkness, and Night
Khonsu God of the Moon
Maat - Goddess of Truth and Order
Mahaf - The Ferryman of the dead
Min - God of Fertility
Montu - Warrior and Sun God
Nefertem - God of the Sunrise
Nehebkau - Joiner of life force to the Body
Nekhbet - Goddess of the Power of Kings
Neith - Goddess of War and Funerals
Nun - Gods of Chaos and Water
Nut - Goddess of the Firmament
Ogdoad - The Creation Gods

Onuris - The War God
Osiris - Lord of the Dead
Qadesh - Goddess of Ecstasy and Sexual Pleasure
Re (Ra) - The Sun God
Renenutet - Goddess of the Harvest
Sebiumeker - God of Procreation
Sefkhet-Abwy - Goddess of Writing
Seshat - Goddess of writing, measurements
Set - God of Evil
Shesmu - Demon god of the Wine Press
Shu - God of the Air and Sky
Taweret - Demon of Birth
Thoth - God of Wisdom
Yamm - God of the Sea

Celtic Gods & Goddesses

Branwyn - Goddess of love, sexuality and the sea -
Bridget - Goddess of fertility, feminine creativity, martial arts and healing
Cernunnos - The 'Horned God of Nature, Animals, Fertility Underworld.
Cerridwen - Moon Goddess, Goddess of Dark Prophecy and Underworld
Coventina - Goddess of Rivers, Abundance, Inspiration and Prophecy- The
Crone - One of the Triple Goddess of Old Age, Winter and Waning Moon.
Eostre - Goddess of Spring, Rebirth, Fertility and New Beginnings -
Epona - Horse Goddess of Prosperity, Healing, Nurturance and Sustenance
Latis - Goddess of Water and Beer -
Lugh - Sun God, God of War, Mastery, Magic and Good Harvest -
Morrigan - Goddess of War, Revenge, Night, Magic and Prophecy. Queen of
Fairies and Witches -

British, Scottish, Irish, Welsh Gods & Goddesses –

Amaethon (Welsh) - God of Agriculture and Magic -
Arawn (Welsh) - God of the Hunt and the Underworld
Arianrhod (Welsh) - Star and Sky Goddess of Beauty, Full Moon and
Magical Spells -
Badb (Irish) - Goddess of War, Death and Rebirth
Caillech (Scottish, Irish, Welsh) - Goddess of Weather, Earth, Sky, Seasons,
Moon and Sun -
Cliodna (Irish, Scottish) - Goddess of Beauty and of Other Realms -
Creide (Irish, Scottish) - Goddess of Women and Fairies

The Green Man (Welsh) - God of the Woodlands, of Life Energy and Fertility -
Morgan LeFay (Welsh) - Goddess of Death, Fate, the Sea and of Curses -
Oghma (Scottish, Irish) - God of Communication and Writing, and of Poets -
Rhiannon (Welsh) - Goddess of Birds, Horses, Enchantments, Fertility and the Underworld -
Skatha (Welsh) - Goddess of the Underworld, Darkness, Magic, Prophecy and Martial Arts -

Chinese Gods & Goddesses

Ch'eng-Huang - God of Moats and Walls –
Kuan Ti - God of War, the Great Judge –
Kwan Yin - Goddess of Mercy and Compassion -
Lei Kun - God of Thunder; chases evil away –
P'an-Chin-Lien - Goddess of Prostitutes -
Ti-Tsang Wang - God of Mercy -
T'shai-shen - God of Wealth
Tsao Wang - God of the Hearth and Family –
Yeng-Wang-Yeh - Lord of Judgment and Death -
Yu-Huang-Shang-Ti - Father the Sky and Heaven -

Greek & Roman Gods and Goddesses

Aphrodite (Greek) - Goddess of Love (Venus) –
Apollo (Greek) - God of Civilization and the Arts -
Ares (Greek) - God of War (Mars) -
Artemis (Greek) - Goddess of birth and Hunt (Diana) -
Athena (Greek) - Goddess of War, Wisdom, Arts (Minerva) -
Ceres (Roman) - Goddess of Agriculture, fertility, and Harvest (Demeter)
Cupid (Roman) - The God of Love
Diana (Roman) - Goddess of the Hunt and Protector of Children (Artemis) -
Dionysos (Greek) - God of Wine -
Eos (Greek) - Goddess of the Dawn and the West Wind
Hades (Greek) - God of the Underworld and the Dead (Pluto) -
Hebe (Greek) - Goddess of Eternal Youth –
Hecate (Greek) - Goddess of the Underworld, Witchcraft and Black Magic –
Hera (Greek) - Goddess of Marriage, Family and Home
Hermes (Greek) - God of Merchants (Mercury) -
Hestia (Greek) - Goddess of Hearth, Fire and Family -
Hypnos (Greek) - God of Sleep -
Jupiter (Roman) - King of the Gods (Zeus) –

Mars (Roman) - God of War (Ares) –
Mercury (Roman) - God of Merchants (Hermes) -
Minerva (Roman) Goddess of Wisdom, War and Crafts (Athena) -
Morpheus (Greek) - God of Dreams –
Nemesis (Greek) - Goddess of Vengeance –
Nike(Greek) - Goddess of Victory –
Persephone (Greek) - Goddess of Fertility and Nature -
Pluto (Roman) - God of the Underworld and the Dead (Hades) -
Poseidon (Greek) - God of Horses, Earthquakes, Storms and the Sea -
Selene (Greek) - Goddess of the Moon
Triton (Greek) - Merman Sea God -
Venus (Roman) - Goddess of Love, Protector of Gardens (Aphrodite) -
Zeus (Greek) - Ruler of the Gods (Jupiter) -

Norse Gods & Goddesses -

Freya - Goddess of Love, Beauty, War, Magic and Wisdom -
Freyr - God of Fertility and Success -
Frigga - Goddess Mother of All, Protector of Children -
Hel - Goddess of the Dead and the Afterlife –
Loki - God of Fire, Trickster God
Odin - God of all Men, Father of all Gods –
Skadi - Goddess of Winter and Hunting –
Thor - God of Sky and Thunder -
Tyr - God of War and Law -

India's Gods & Goddesses -

Brahma - God of the Triniity -
Durga - Goddess beyond reach; also known as Shakti (Life Energy) and
Parvati (Family Unity) -
Ganesha - God who Removes Obstacles, God of Knowledge -
Gauri - Goddess of Purity and Austerity –
Hanuman - Monkey God, provider of Courage, Hope, Knowledge, Intellect
and Devotion -
Kali - Goddess of Destruction -Krishna - God of Power and Bravery -
Lakshmi - Goddess of Prosperity, Purity, Chastity, and Generosity -
Rama - Hero, Preserver of Families, Destroyer of Evil -
Sarasvati - Goddess of Speech, Wisdom and Learning -
Shiva - God of Giving and Happiness, Creator -
Vishnu - God of Courage, Knowledge and Power; Also known as Hari the
Remover -

Sumerian Gods & Goddesses -

An - God of the Heavens -
Enki - Lord of Water and Wisdom –
Enlil - God of Air and Storms -
Ereshkigal - Goddess of Darkness, Gloom and Death -
Inanna - Goddess of Love and War -
Ki - Goddess of the Earth -
Nammu - Goddess of the Sea -
Ninhursag - Goddess of the Earth, Fertility –
Utu - Sun God, God of Justice -

African Gods & Goddesses

Amun - King of the Gods -
Ani-lbo - Goddess of Birth, Death, Happiness and Love
Anubis - God of the Dead -
Atum - First God, God of Perfection -
Bastet - Goddess of Protection -
Bes - Goddess of Childbirth and Family; Protection for Children, Pregnant
Women and Families -
Geb - God of the Earth -
Hathor - Goddess of Love and Joy -
Horus - God of the Sky, Ruler of Egypt -
Isis - Goddess of Protection and Magic -
Leza - Creator who is Compassionate and Merciful (Rhodesia) -
Ma'at - Goddess of Truth, Justice and Harmony -
Nephthys - Goddess of the Dead -
Ngai - High God, Creator and Giver of All Things
Nun - God of Water and Chaos -
Nut - Goddess of the Sky who Covers the Earth -
Nzambi - Unapproachable God, Sovereign Master -
Obatala - Goddess of Earth and People, Creator -
Osiris - God of the Dead, Ruler of the Underworld -
Ra - Sun God -
Raluvhimba - God of the Heavens, Creator
Seshat - Goddess of Writing and Measurement -

Seth - God of Chaos -
Thoth - God of Writing and Knowledge –
Wadjet - Cobra Goddess, Protector of the King –

Appendix "B"

The following list is of traditional angel names gathered from different religions, mythologies and lore. These angels are those considered to good and not fallen angels or demons.

Abasdarhon - angel of the fifth hour of the night.
Abraxos - ancient name attributed to an angel.
Adnachiel - angel who rules November.
Adonael - an archangel.
Adonai - one of seven angels of the presence, or elohim; creator.
Aeshma - Persian archangel.
Af - angel of light.
Agla - angel who saved Lot and his family.
Akriel - angel who aids those with infertility.
Amitiel - angel of truth.
Amriel - angel of the month of May.
Anael - angel influencing love, passion and sexuality.
Anapiel - angel whose name means "branch of God."
Anahel - angel who rules the third heaven.
Anpiel - angel who protects birds.
Ansiel - name of an angel known as "the constrainer."
Arael - variation of Uriel; prince over the people.
Araqiel - angel with dominion over the earth.
Araton - one of seven ruling angels over the provinces of heaven.
Ariel - "lion of God;" angel of protection.
Armisael - angel of the womb.
Asariel - "whom God has bound;" rules the moon.
Asroilu - guardian angel of the seventh heaven.
Astanphaeus - one of the seven angels of the presence; third gate guardian.
Asteraoth - name of an angel who thwarts power.
Atrugiel - great prince of the seventh heaven.
Ayil - angel of the zodiac sign Sagittarius.
Azbogah - name of the high ranking angel of judgment.
Azrael - archangel of death.
Azriel - name for the angel of destruction.
Balthioul - angel with the power to thwart distress.
Baradiel - angel of hail.
Barakiel - angel of lightning.
Barrattiel - angel of support.
Barbiel - angel of October.
Bariel - ruling angel of the eleventh hour of the day.

Barman - angel of intelligence.
Barquiel - ruling angel of the seventh hour of the day.
Baruchiel - angel with power over strife.
Bath Kol - female angel of divine prophecy.
Bazazath - archangel of the second heaven.
Bethor - one of seven ruling angels of the province of heaven.
Briathos - name of an angel who thwarts demons.
Cahethal - seraphim angel over agriculture.
Camael - angel name that means "he who sees God;" chief angel of powers.
Cassiel - angel of Saturn.
Cerviel - angel ruler of the principalities.
Chamuel - archangel whose name means "he who seeks God."
Chayyliel - angel whose name means "army;" a powerful angel.
Cochabiel - angel prince who stands before God.
Dabriel - angel of the first heaven who rules over Monday.
Dagiel - angel who has dominion over fish.
Dalquiel - angel prince of the third heaven.
Damabiath - angel of naval construction.
Dardariel - ruling angel of the eleventh hour.
Diniel - angel who protects infants.
Domiel - angel who guards the sixth hall of the seventh heaven.
Dubbiel - guardian angel of Persia; name means "bear-God."
Duma - angel prince of dreams.
Dumah - angel of silence.
Eae - angel who thwarts demons.
Eiael - angel with dominion over the occult sciences.
Elyon - ministering angel who brought the plague of hail upon Egypt.
Emmanuel - angel whose name means "God with us."
Erathaol - one of seven great archon angels.
Eremiel - great angel who presides over the Abyss and Hades.
Gabriel - archangel whose name means "man or hero of God."
Gadriel - angel who rules the fifth heaven.
Galgaliel - prince angel of the sun, like Raphael.
Galizur - great angel who rules the second heaven.
Gamaliel - angel who takes the elect unto heaven.
Gazardiel - angel who supervises the east.
Geburatiel - angel prince who guards the seventh heaven.
Guriel - angel of the zodiac sign of Leo.
Gzrel - angel who revokes any evil decree against another in heaven.
Hadraniel - angel standing at the second gate in heaven; "majesty of God."
Hadriel - guardian angel of the gates of the east wind.
Hagith - one of the seven ruling angels of the provinces of heaven.
Halaliel - archangel known as "the lord of karma."
Hamaliel - angel who rules the order of virtues.

Hamon - a great, honored, beautiful prince angel in heaven.
Haniel - an archangel who guards the tree of life.
Harahel - angel who oversees libraries.
Hasdiel - angel of benevolence.
Hasmal - fire speaking angel of the throne of God.
Hayliel - angel prince in the seventh heaven.
Haziel - angel whose name means "vision of God."
Heman - angel leader of the heavenly choir, whose name means "trust."
Hermesiel - angel who leads one of the heavenly choirs.
Hofniel - ruling angel of the bene elohim; name means "fighter of God."
Iaoel - an angel of the lord; angel of visions.
Iaoth - archangel who has power to thwart demons.
Leo - an angel who thwarts demons.
Iofiel - archangel whose name means "beauty of God."
Israfil - Islamic angel whose name means "the burning one."
Jael - cherub who guards the ark of the covenant.
Jahoel - one of the angels of the presence and chief of the seraphim.
Jaoel - guardian angel who lives in the seventh heaven.
Jeduthun – angel, name means "master of howling" or chanting to God.
Jefischa - ruling angel of the fourth hour of the night.
Jehudiel - archangel who rules the movements of the heavenly spheres.
Jeremiel - archangel whose name means "mercy of God."
Kabshiel - angel of grace and favor.
Kafziel - archangel who rules the planet Saturn.
Kakabel - angel who rules over stars and constellations.
Kalaziel - angel who has the power to thwart demons of disease.
Karael - angel who has the power to thwart demons.
Kemuel - archon angel and chief of the seraphim.
Kerubiel - prince angel of the cherubim.
Kokabiel - prince angel of the stars.
Kutiel - angel of water and the use of diving rods.
Labbiel - angel whose name was changed to Raphael.
Lahabiel - angel who protects against evil spirits.
Lamechial - angel who thwarts deception.
Lassuarium - angel who rules the tenth hour of the night.
Laylah - angel who oversees and protects childbirth.
Machidiel - angel governing the zodiac sign of Aries, the month of March.
Marmaroth - angel who has power to thwart fate.
Mendrion - angel who rules the seventh hour of the night.
Metatron - one of the greatest archangels, second only to God.
Michael - great archangel whose name means "who is as God."
Mihr - angel of divine mercy; angel that governs September.
Miniel - angel invoked to induce love.
Mitatron - an angel of the third heaven.

Morael - angel of awe that rules the months of August-September.
Moroni - brought messages to Joseph Smith, founder of Mormonism.
Muriel - angel who rules the dominions and the month of June.
Naaririel - great prince angel of the seventh heaven.
Nahaliel - angel who governs running streams; "valley of God."
Nanael - angel who governs the sciences, and philosophy.
Narcariel - angel that rules the eighth hour of the night.
Nasargiel - good angel with a lion head that rules hell.
Nathanael - angel ruling over hidden things, fire and vengeance.
Naya'il - angel of testing.
Nelchael - angel of the schemhamphorae.
Nuriel - angel of spellbinding power and of hail storms.
Och - one ruling angel of the provinces of heaven.
Omael - angel of chemistry and species perpetuation.
Onoel - name of an archon angel...
Ophaniel - prince angel over the ophanim.
Ophiel - one ruling angel of the provinces of heaven and Mercury.
Oriel - ruling angel of the tenth hour of the day.
Orifiel - archangel over thrones, and the second hour of the day.
Orphamiel - angel known as the "great finger of the Father."
Osmadiel - ruling angel of the eighth hour of the day.
Ouriel - archangel who commands demons.
Pamyel - ruling angel of the ninth hour of night.
Pathiel - angel whose name means "opener of God."
Peliel - angel who rules the virtues.
Peniel - angel who rules Friday and resides in the third heaven.
Pesagniyah - angel who ushers prayers of grief to heaven.
Phaleg - one of the seven ruling angels of the provinces of heaven.
Phanuel - archangel who is an interpreter of revelations.
Phounebiel - disease thwarting angel.
Phul one of the seven ruling angels of the provinces of heaven.
Pravuil - an archangel who keeps all the records of heaven.
Pronoia - an archon angel who helped make mankind.
Purah - angel of forgetfulness.
Puriel - angel whose name means "the fire of God;" angel of punishment.
Qaspiel - angel who rules the moon.
Quabriel - ruling angel of the ninth hour of the day.
Rachiel - ophanim angel who rules Venus and governs sexuality.
Rachmiel - angel of mercy whose name also means the same.
Radueriel - angel who can create other angels and oversees archives.
Raguel - angel who watches over the behavior of angels; "friend of God."
Rahab - angel of death, destruction, but also the sea.
Rahatiel - angel prince of the constellations; name means "to run."
Rahmiel - angel of mercy and love.

Ramiel - angel who oversees visions and souls during the day of judgment.
Raphael - great archangel whose name means "the shining one who heals."
Rathanael - angel of the third heaven and thwarter of demons.
Raziel - angel chief over the thrones, guarding the secrets of the universe.
Remiel - angel who leads souls to judgment; name means "mercy of God."
Rikbiel - angel who oversees the divine chariot; chief of wheels.
Rizoel - angel with power to thwart demons.
Rogziel - angel of punishment whose name means "the wrath of God."
Ruman - angel who takes account of evil men's deeds while in hell.
Sabaoth - archon angel of the presence.
Sabathiel - angel or intelligence who communicates divine light.
Sablo - angel of graciousness and protection.
Sabrael - archangel who guards the first heaven.
Sabrathan - ruling angel of the first hour of the night.
Sachiel - ruling angel of Jupiter whose name means "covering of God."
Sagnessagiel - angel who guards the fourth hall of the seventh heaven.
Sahaqiel - angel prince of the fourth heaven.
Salathiel - rescuing angel of Adam and Eve.
Samkiel - angel of destruction and purifier of souls from sheol.
Samuel - Ruling angel of the first hour of the day.
Sandalphon - giant angel whose name means "co-brother" (of Metratron).
Saniel - ruling angel of the sixth hour of the day.
Sarakiel - angel who rules the ministering angels.
Sarandiel - ruling angel of the twelfth hour of the night.
Satqiel - angel prince of the fifth heaven.
Seraphiel - chief angel of the seraphim angels.
Shamsiel - angel whose name means "light of day."
Shepherd - angel of repentance.
Shoftiel - angel whose name means "the judge of God."
Sidqiel - angel prince of the ophanim; ruler of Venus.
Sidriel - angel prince of the first heaven.
Simiel - archangel.
Sizouze - angel of prayer.
Sophia - angel whose name means "wisdom."
Soqedhozi - angel who weighs the merits of of men before God.
Sorath - angel who is the spirit of the sun.
Sorush - angel who punishes souls on judgment day.
Soterasiel - angel whose name means "who stirs up the fire of God."
Sraosha - angel who sets the world in motion.
Suriel - angel of healing whose name means "God's command."
Tagas - governing angel of singing angels.
Tartys - ruling angel of the second hour of the night.
Tatrasiel - great angelic prince.
Temeluch - angel caretaker who protects newborn babies and children.

Temperance - angel of the elixir of life.
Theliel - angel prince of love.
Tubiel - angel of summer.
Tzadkiel - angel of justice and guardian of the gates of the east wind.
Ubaviel - angel of the zodiac sign of Capricorn.
Umabel - angel of physics and astronomy.
Uriel - great archangel whose name means "God is my light."
Usiel - an angel who stands before the throne of God.
Uzziel - cherubim angel whose name means "strength of God."
Varhmiel - ruling angel of the fourth hour of the day.
Vequaniel - ruling angel of the third hour of the day.
Verchiel - ruling angel of the month of July and of the zodiac sign Leo.
Vretiel - swift in wisdom archangel responsible for recording God's deeds.
Xathanael - the sixth angel created by God.
Yabbashael - an angel of the earth whose name means "the mainland."
Yefefiah - archangel who is the prince of the Torah.
Yehudiah - benevolent angel of death.
Yerachmiel - an archangel who rules earth.
Yeshamiel - angel who rules the zodiac sign of Libra.
Yofiel - angel prince of the Torah commanding 53 legions of angels.
Zaapiel - angel punisher of wicked souls.
Zaazenach - ruling angel of the sixth hour of the night.
Zabkiel - angel who rules over the thrones.
Zachariel - angel governor of Jupiter.
Zachriel - angel who governs memories.
Zadkeil - archangel who rules heaven and stands in the presence of God.
Zagzagel - angel prince of the Torah and of wisdom.
Zakzakiel - angel of the seventh heaven who records good deeds.
Zaphiel - angel ruler of the cherubim.
Zaphkiel - archangel whose name means "knowledge of God."
Zarall - cherub angel who guards the ark of the covenant.
Zazriel - angel whose name means "strength of God."
Zehanpuryu - high ranking angel whose name means "one who sets free."
Zerachiel - angel of the month of July and the sun.
Zophiel - angel whose name means "God's spy."
Zuriel - ruler of the principalities whose name means "my rock is God."

Evil Angels, Fallen Angels, or Demons:

AGLÆCA: An Old English dictionary defines áglaeca as follows: "wretch, miscreant, monster, demon, fierce enemy, fierce combatant, miserable being." In the Anglo-Saxon epic Beowulf, Grendel, Grendel's mother and Beowulf are all three referred to by this name for each is a "fierce combatant." Variant spelling of Anglo-Saxon unisex Aglæca, meaning both "demon, monster, fiend," and "hero, warrior."

NUKPANA: Native American Hopi unisex name meaning "evil."

ABADDON : Greek name derived from Hebrew abaddown, meaning "destruction, ruination." In the New Testament bible, this is the name of the place of destruction. And it is a name given to the angel of the bottomless pit, the Destroyer Apollyon. An Anglicized form of Greek Abaddon, meaning "destruction, ruination." In the New Testament bible, this is the name of the place of destruction. And it is a name given to the angel of the bottomless pit, the Destroyer Apollyon.

ADDANC: In Welsh legend, this is the name of a lake monster that King Arthur (or Percival) killed. It is variously described as a demon, a dwarf, beaver, or crocodile. It was said to prey upon anyone foolish enough to swim in its lake.

AHRIMAN: Middle Persian form of Old Persian Angra Mainyu, meaning "devil; evil spirit." In mythology, this is the name of the god of darkness, death and destruction, and the number one enemy of Ahura Mazda.

ALIAH: Variant of Hebrew Alvah (having the letters transposed), meaning "evil, iniquity." In the bible, this is the name of a duke of Edom.

ALVA: Variant spelling of Hebrew Alvah, meaning "evil, iniquity." Compare with feminine forms of Alva.

ALVAH: Hebrew name meaning "evil, iniquity." In the bible, this is the name of a duke of Edom. Also spelled Aliah.

ANGRA MAINYU: Old Persian myth name of the source of all evil, the twin brother and main enemy of Ahura Mazda, meaning "evil spirit; devil."

APEP: Egyptian name, possibly connected to the root pp, meaning "to slither." In mythology, Apep is the personification of evil, seen as a giant snake, serpent or dragon. Known as the Serpent of the Nile or Evil Lizard, he was an enemy of the sun god.

AZA'ZEL: Hebrew word meaning "entire removal" and "scapegoat." In the bible, this word is found in the law of the day of atonement (Leviticus 16:8, 10, 26). It refers to a goat used for sacrifice for the sins of the people. In modern times, Azazel was interpreted as a Satanic, goat-like demon. The name has even been used for the "Angel of Death."

AZAZEL: Anglicized form of Hebrew Aza'zel, meaning "entire removal" and "scapegoat." In the bible, this word is found in the law of the day of atonement (Leviticus 16:8, 10, 26). It refers to a goat used for sacrifice for the sins of the people. In modern times, Azazel was interpreted as a Satanic, goat-like demon. The name has even been used for the "Angel of Death."

CERBERUS: Latin form of Greek Kerberos, meaning "demon of the pit." In mythology, this is the name of the three-headed dog that guards the entrance to Hades.

ⵏERNOBOG: Czech form of Russian Chernobog, meaning "black god." In Slavic mythology, this is the name of a god of evil and darkness, the counterpart of Belobog ("white god").

CHERNOBOG: Russian form of Slavic Crnobog, composed of the elements cherno "black" and bog "god," hence "black god." In Slavic mythology, this is the name of a god of evil and darkness, the counterpart of Belobog ("white god").

CRNOBOG: Variant form of Russian Czernobog, meaning "black god." In mythology, this is the name of a god of evil and darkness, the counterpart of Belobog ("white god").

CZERNOBOG: Russian form of Slavic Zherneboh, meaning "black god."

DEMOGORGON: Greek myth name of a god of the underworld, thought to be a name for Satan, possibly composed of the Greek elements daimon "demon, devil" and gorgos "grim," hence "grim demon."

DEMON: Ancient Greek name derived from the word demos, meaning "the people."

DEVIL: English form of Greek Diabolos, meaning "accuser, slanderer." In the bible, this is a title for Satan, the prince of demons and author of evil, who estranges men from God and entices them to sin. Figuratively, the devil is a man who, by opposing the cause of God, may be said to act the part of the devil or to side with him.

DIABOLOS: Greek name meaning "accuser, slanderer." In the bible, this is a title for Satan, the prince of demons and author of evil, who estranges men from God and entices them to sin. Figuratively, the devil is a man who, by opposing the cause of God, may be said to act the part of the devil or to side with him.

DRACUL: Romanian name meaning "devil" or "dragon."

KARAWAN: An expression used to avert the evil eye, transferred to forename use.

KERBEROS: Greek name meaning "demon of the pit." In mythology, this is the name of the three-headed dog that guards the entrance to Hades.

MATCHITEHEW: Native American Algonquin name meaning "he has an evil heart."

MUKESH: Hindi myth name of a demon in the form of a boar who was killed by Shiva, meaning "ruler of Muka."

NAZAR: Turkish name derived from the word nazar, the name of an amulet known as the "evil eye stone" used to ward off evil. Compare with another form of Nazar.

RAVANA: Hindi name meaning "person with ten necks." In Hindu mythology, this is the name of a demon king of Ceylon who kidnapped Rama's wife, Sita.

SAMA'EL: Variant spelling of Hebrew Samael, the name of an Angel of Death, meaning "whom God makes" and "venom of God."

SAMAEL: In Jewish mythology, this is the name of an archangel, a fallen angel, the Angel of Death or Poison, the accuser, seducer, and destroyer famously known as The Grim Reaper. He is said to be both good and evil, having been one of the heavenly host. He rules over seven habitations called Sheba Ha-yechaloth, infernal realms of the Earth. The Talmud states: "the evil Spirit, Satan, and Sama'el the Angel of Death, are the same"; and Samael is also therein equated with the biblical serpent who tempted Eve in the Garden of Eden. He is called the Prince of Darkness and chief of the Dragons of Evil and is held responsible for the scorching wind of the desert called the simoom. It is probably the Hebrew form of Syrian Shemal ("left"), but composed of 'el "god" and suwm "to create" or "to place, to set," hence "whom God makes." It is also sometimes rendered "venom of God." Also spelled Samil and Sammael.

SAMIL: Variant form of Hebrew Samael, the name of an Angel of Death, meaning "whom God makes" and "venom of God."

SAMMAEL: Variant spelling of Hebrew Samael, the name of an Angel of Death, meaning "whom God makes" and "venom of God."

SATAN: Greek form of Hebrew satan, meaning "adversary." In the bible, this is the name of the inveterate enemy of God. In the New Testament, Hebrew satan is translated once into Greek Diabolos, and once using the word epiboulos, meaning "plotter." This is also the Late Latin and Old English form of Hebrew satan.

SATANAS: Greek name of Aramaic origin, corresponding to Greek Satan, from Hebrew satan, meaning "adversary." In the bible, this is the name of the inveterate enemy of God.

SET: Another form of Egyptian Sutekh, possibly meaning "one who dazzles." In mythology, this is the name of an ancient evil god of Chaos, storms, and the desert, who slew Osiris.

SETH: Greek form of Egyptian Set, possibly meaning "one who dazzles." In mythology, this is the name of an ancient evil god of Chaos, storms, and the desert, who slew Osiris. Compare with other forms of Seth.

SETHOS: Greek form of Egyptian Sutekh, possibly meaning "one who dazzles." In mythology, this is the name of an ancient evil god of Chaos, storms, and the desert, who slew Osiris.

SHEMAL: Syrian name meaning "left." In mythology, this is the name of the Lord of the genii and demons.

SUTEKH: Egyptian name, possibly meaning "one who dazzles." In mythology, this is the name of an ancient evil god of Chaos, storms, and the desert, who slew Osiris.

TEIVEL: Yiddish name meaning "devil."

TJERNOBOG: Danish form of Slavic Crnobog, meaning "black god." In Slavic mythology, this is the name of a god of evil and darkness, the counterpart of Belobog ("white god").

TⲖERNOBOG: Finnish form of Slavic Crnobog, meaning "black god." In Slavic mythology, this is the name of a god of evil and darkness, the counterpart of Belobog ("white god").

VRITRA: Hindi myth name of a dragon or serpent, the personification of drought and enemy of Indra, meaning "the enveloper."

ZERNEBOG: Variant form of Russian Czernobog, meaning "black god."

ZHERNEBOH: Slavic name meaning "black god."

ZLOGONJE: Slavic name meaning "expels evil."

Female Demons:

HECATE: Latin form of Greek Hekate, meaning "worker from far off." In mythology, this is the name of a goddess of witchcraft, demons, graves, and the underworld.

HEKATE : Variant spelling of Greek Hekabe, meaning "worker from far off." In mythology, this is the name of a goddess of witchcraft, demons, graves, and the underworld.

IEZABEL : Greek form of Hebrew Iyzebel ("Ba'al exalts," "unchaste," or "without cohabitation"), but meaning "chaste, intact." In the bible, this is the name of the evil wife of King Ahab. She was eaten by dogs as prophesied by Elijah.

IYZEBEL: Hebrew name meaning "Ba'al exalts," "unchaste," or "without cohabitation." In the bible, this is the name of the evil wife of King Ahab. She was eaten by dogs as prophesied by Elijah.

JEZEBEL: Anglicized form of Hebrew Iyzebel ("Ba'al exalts," "unchaste," or "without cohabitation") and Greek Iezabel ("chaste, intact"). In the bible, this is the name of the evil wife of King Ahab. She was eaten by dogs as prophesied by Elijah.

LAMIA: Greek myth name of an evil spirit who abducts and devours children, meaning "large shark." The name means "vampire" in Latin and "fiend" in Arabic.

LILIT: Variant spelling of Hebrew Lilith, meaning "of the night."

LILITH: Hebrew form of Sumerian Lilitu, meaning "of the night." In mythology, this is the name of a Mesopotamian storm demon associated with the wind and thought to bear disease and death. In ancient Semitic folklore, it is the name of a night demon. The oldest story considers Lilith to be Adam's first wife. In the bible, this is simply a word for a "screech owl."

LILITU: Sumerian name meaning "of the night."

PANDORA: Greek name composed of the elements pan "all" and doron "gift," hence "all-gift." In mythology, this is the name of the first mortal woman whose curiosity unleashed evil into the world.

USHA: Female Hindi myth name of a demon princess, daughter of heaven, and sister of night, meaning "dawn."

Appendix "C"

Verses Addressing Angels and Archangels.

New testament:

Genesis 19:1   The two angels reached Sodom in the evening, as Lot was sitting at the gate of Sodom. When Lot saw them, he got up to greet them; and bowing down with his face to the ground,

Genesis 19:12   Then the angels said to Lot: "Who else belongs to you here? Your sons (sons-in-law) and your daughters and all who belong to you in the city--take them away from it!

Genesis 19:15   As dawn was breaking, the angels urged Lot on, saying, "On your way! Take with you your wife and your two daughters who are here, or you will be swept away in the punishment of the city."

Genesis 48:16   The Angel who has delivered me from all harm, bless these boys that in them my name be recalled, and the names of my fathers, Abraham and Isaac, and they may become teeming multitudes upon the earth!"

Exodus 3:2   There an angel of the LORD appeared to him in fire flaming out of a bush. As he looked on, he was surprised to see that the bush, though on fire, was not consumed.

Exodus 14:19   The angel of God, who had been leading Israel's camp, now moved and went around behind them. The column of cloud also, leaving the front, took up its place behind them,

Exodus 23:20   "See, I am sending an angel before you, to guard you on the way and bring you to the place I have prepared.

Exodus 23:23   "My angel will go before you and bring you to the Amorites, Hittites, Perizzites, Canaanites, Hivites and Jebusites; and I will wipe them out.

Exodus 32:34   Now, go and lead the people whither I have told you. My angel will go before you. When it is time for me to punish, I will punish them for their sin."

Exodus 33:2   Driving out the Canaanites, Amorites, Hittites, Perizzites, Hivites and Jebusites, I will send an angel before you

Numbers 20:16   and how, when we cried to the LORD, he heard our cry and sent an angel who led us out of Egypt. Now here we are at the town of Kadesh at the edge of your territory.

Numbers 22:22-27   But now the anger of God flared up at him for going, and the angel of the LORD stationed himself on the road to hinder him as he was riding along on his ass, accompanied by two of his servants. [23] When the ass saw the angel of the LORD standing on the road with sword drawn, she turned off the road and went into the field, and Balaam had to beat her to bring her back on the road. [24] Then the angel of the LORD took his stand in a narrow lane between vineyards with a stone wall on each side. [25] When the ass saw the angel of the LORD there, she shrank against the wall; and since she squeezed Balaam's leg against it, he beat her again. [26] The angel of the LORD then went ahead, and stopped next in a passage so narrow that there was no room to move either to the right or to the left. [27] When the ass saw the angel of the LORD there, she cowered under Balaam. So, in anger, he again beat the ass with his stick.

Numbers 22:31-32   Then the LORD removed the veil from Balaam's eyes, so that he too saw the angel of the LORD standing on the road with sword drawn; and he fell on his knees and bowed to the ground. [32] But the angel of the LORD said to him, "Why have you beaten your ass these three times? It is I who have come armed to hinder you because this rash journey of yours is directly opposed to me.

Numbers 22:34-35   Then Balaam said to the angel of the LORD, "I have sinned. Yet I did not know that you stood against me to oppose my journey. Since it has displeased you, I will go back home." [35] But the angel of the LORD said to Balaam, "Go with the men; but you may say only what I tell you." So Balaam went on with the princes of Balak.

Deut. 32:43   Exult with him, you heavens, glorify him, all you angels of God;   For he avenges the blood of his servants and purges his people's land.

Judges 2:1   An angel of the LORD went up from Gilgal to Bochim and said, "It was I who brought you up from Egypt and led you into the land which I promised on oath to your fathers. I said that I would never break my covenant with you,

Judges 2:4   When the angel of the LORD had made these threats to all the Israelites, the people wept aloud;

Judges 6:11-12   Then the angel of the LORD came and sat under the terebinth in Ophrah that belonged to Joash the Abiezrite. While his son Gideon was beating out wheat in the wine press to save it from the Midianites, [12] the angel of the LORD appeared to him and said, "The LORD is with you, O champion!"

Judges 6:20-22   The angel of God said to him, "Take the meat and unleavened cakes and lay them on this rock; then pour out the broth." When he had done so, [21] the angel of the LORD stretched out the tip of the staff he held, and touched the meat and unleavened cakes. Thereupon a fire came up from the rock which consumed the meat and unleavened cakes, and the angel of the LORD disappeared from sight. [22] Gideon, now aware that it had been the angel of the LORD, said, "Alas, Lord GOD, that I have seen the angel of the LORD face to face!"

Judges 13:3   An angel of the LORD appeared to the woman and said to her, "Though you are barren and have had no children, yet you will conceive and bear a son.

Judges 13:6   The woman went and told her husband, "A man of God came to me; he had the appearance of an angel of God, terrible indeed. I did not ask him where he came from, nor did he tell me his name.

Judges 13:9   God heard the prayer of Manoah, and the angel of God came again to the woman as she was sitting in the field. Since her husband Manoah was not with her,

Judges 13:13　　The angel of the LORD answered Manoah, "Your wife is to abstain from all the things of which I spoke to her.

Judges 13:15-16　　Then Manoah said to the angel of the LORD, "Can we persuade you to stay, while we prepare a kid for you?" [16] But the angel of the LORD answered Manoah, "Although you press me, I will not partake of your food. But if you will, you may offer a holocaust to the LORD."Not knowing that it was the angel of the LORD,

Judges 13:18　　The angel of the LORD answered him, "Why do you ask my name, which is mysterious?"

Judges 13:20-21　　as the flame rose to the sky from the altar, the angel of the LORD ascended in the flame of the altar. When Manoah and his wife saw this, they fell prostrate to the ground; [21] but the angel of the LORD was seen no more by Manoah and his wife. Then Manoah, realizing that it was the angel of the LORD,

1 Samuel 29:10　　So the first thing tomorrow, you and your lord's servants who came with you, go to the place I picked out for you. Do not decide to take umbrage at this; you are as acceptable to me as an angel of God. But make an early morning start, as soon as it grows light, and be on your way."

2 Samuel 14:17　　And the woman concluded: "Let the word of my lord the king provide a resting place; indeed, my lord the king is like an angel of God, evaluating good and bad. The LORD your God be with you."

2 Samuel 14:20　　Your servant Joab did this to come at the issue in a roundabout way. But my lord is as wise as an angel of God, so that he knows all things on earth."

2 Samuel 19:27　　[28] But he slandered your servant before my lord the king. But my lord the king is like an angel of God. Do what you judge best.

2 Samuel 24:16-17   But when the angel stretched forth his hand toward Jerusalem to destroy it, the LORD regretted the calamity and said to the angel causing the destruction among the people, "Enough now! Stay your hand." The angel of the LORD was then standing at the threshing floor of Araunah the Jebusite. [17] When David saw the angel who was striking the people, he said to the LORD: "It is I who have sinned; it is I, the shepherd, who have done wrong. But these are sheep; what have they done? Punish me and my kindred."

1 Kings 13:18   But he said to him, "I, too, am a prophet like you, and an angel told me in the word of the LORD to bring you back with me to my house and to have you eat bread and drink water." He was lying to him, however.

1 Kings 19:5   He lay down and fell asleep under the broom tree, but then an angel touched him and ordered him to get up and eat.

1 Kings 19:7   but the angel of the LORD came back a second time, touched him, and ordered, "Get up and eat, else the journey will be too long for you!"

2 Kings 1:3   Meanwhile, the angel of the LORD said to Elijah the Tishbite: "Go, intercept the messengers of Samaria's king, and ask them, 'Is it because there is no God in Israel that you are going to inquire of Baalzebub, the god of Ekron?'

2 Kings 1:15   Then the angel of the LORD said to Elijah, "Go down with him; you need not be afraid of him."

2 Kings 19:35   That night the angel of the LORD went forth and struck down one hundred and eighty-five thousand men in the Assyrian camp. Early the next morning, there they were, all the corpses of the dead.

1 Chron. 12:22   [23] And from day to day men kept coming to David's help until there was a vast encampment, like an encampment of angels.

1 Chron. 21:12   will it be three years of famine; or three months of fleeing your enemies, with the sword of your foes ever at your back; or three days

of the LORD'S own sword, a pestilence in the land, with the LORD'S destroying angel in every part of Israel? Therefore choose: What answer am I to give him who sent me?"

1 Chron. 21:15-16   God also sent an angel to destroy Jerusalem; but as he was on the point of destroying it, the LORD saw and decided against the calamity, and said to the destroying angel, "Enough now! Stay your hand!" The angel of the LORD was then standing by the threshing floor of Ornan the Jebusite. [16] When David raised his eyes, he saw the angel of the LORD standing between earth and heaven, with a naked sword in his hand stretched out against Jerusalem. David and the elders, clothed in sackcloth, prostrated themselves face to the ground,

1 Chron. 21:18   Then the angel of the LORD commanded Gad to tell David to go up and erect an altar to the LORD on the threshing floor of Ornan the Jebusite.

1 Chron. 21:27   Then the LORD gave orders to the angel to return his sword to its sheath.

1 Chron. 21:30   But David could not go there to worship God, for he was fearful of the sword of the angel of the LORD.

2 Chron. 32:21   Then the LORD sent an angel, who destroyed every valiant warrior, leader and commander in the camp of the Assyrian king, so that he had to return shamefaced to his own country. And when he entered the temple of his god, some of his own offspring struck him down there with the sword.

Tobit 5:4   Tobiah went to look for someone acquainted with the roads who would travel with him to Media. As soon as he went out, he found the angel Raphael standing before him, though he did not know that this was an angel of God.

Tobit 5:17   Tobit said, "God bless you, brother." Then he called his son and said to him: "My son, prepare whatever you need for the journey, and set out with your kinsman. May God in heaven protect you on the way and bring you back to me safe and sound; and may his angel accompany you for safety, my son." Before setting out on his journey, Tobiah kissed his father and mother. Tobit said to him, "Have a safe journey."

Tobit 5:22-6:1 [22b] For a good angel will go with him, his journey will be successful, and he will return unharmed." [6:1] Then she stopped weeping.

[2a] When the boy left home, accompanied by the angel, Tobit 6:4-5 But the angel said to him, "Take hold of the fish and don't let it get away!" The boy seized the fish and hauled it up on the shore. [5] The angel then told him: "Cut the fish open and take out its gall, heart, and liver, and keep them with you; but throw away the entrails. Its gall, heart, and liver make useful medicines." Tobit 6:7 [7b] The boy asked the angel this question: "Brother Azariah, what medicinal value is there in the fish's heart, liver, and gall?"

Tobit 11:14 and wept. He exclaimed, "I can see you, son, the light of my eyes!" Then he said: "Blessed be God, and praised be his great name, and blessed be all his holy angels. May his holy name be praised throughout all the ages,   Tobit 12:15 I am Raphael, one of the seven angels who enter and serve before the Glory of the Lord." Tobit 12:22 They kept thanking God and singing his praises; and they continued to acknowledge these marvelous deeds which he had done when the angel of God appeared to them.

Esth. 11:13   [D:13] She replied: "I saw you, my lord, as an angel of God, and my heart was troubled with fear of your majesty.

1 Macc. 7:41   "When they who were sent by the king blasphemed, your angel went out and killed a hundred and eighty-five thousand of them.

2 Macc. 11:6   When Maccabeus and his men learned that Lysias was besieging the strongholds, they and all the people begged the Lord with lamentations and tears to send a good angel to save Israel.

2 Macc. 15:22-23   He prayed to him thus: "You, O LORD, sent your angel in the days of King Hezekiah of Judea, and he slew a hundred and eighty-

five thousand men of Sennacherib's army. [23] Sovereign of the heavens, send a good angel now to spread fear and dread before us.

Job 4:18   Lo, he puts no trust in his servants, and with his angels he can find fault.

Job 33:23   If then there be for him an angel, one out of a thousand, a mediator, to show him what is right for him and bring the man back to justice,

Psalm 34:7   [8] The angel of the LORD, who encamps with them, delivers all who fear God.

Psalm 35:5-6   Make them like chaff before the wind, with the angel of the LORD driving them on.   [6] Make their way slippery and dark, with the angel of the LORD pursuing them.

Psalm 91:11   For God commands the angels to guard you in all your ways.

Psalm 103:20   Bless the LORD, all you angels, mighty in strength and attentive, obedient to every command.

Psalm 148:2   Praise him, all you angels; give praise, all you hosts.

Wisdom 16:20   Instead of this, you nourished your people with food of angels and furnished them bread from heaven, ready to hand, untoiled-for, endowed with all delights and conforming to every taste.

Isaiah 37:36   The angel of the LORD went forth and struck down one hundred and eighty-five thousand in the Assyrian camp. Early the next morning, there they were, all the corpses of the dead.

Isaiah 63:9 in their every affliction. It was not a messenger or an angel, but he himself who saved them. Because of his love and pity he redeemed them himself, lifting them and carrying them all the days of old.

Baruch 6:6 for my angel is with you, and he is the custodian of your lives.

Daniel 3:28   [95] Nebuchadnezzar exclaimed, "Blessed be the God of Shadrach, Meshach, and Abednego, who sent his angel to deliver the servants that trusted in him; they disobeyed the royal command and yielded their bodies rather than serve or worship any god except their own God.

Daniel 3:49 But the angel of the Lord went down into the furnace with Azariah and his companions, drove the fiery flames out of the furnace, Daniel 3:58 Angels of the Lord, bless the Lord, praise and exalt him above all forever.

Daniel 6:22   [23] My God has sent his angel and closed the lions' mouths so that they have not hurt me. For I have been found innocent before him; neither to you have I done any harm, O king!"

Daniel 13:55b "Your fine lie has cost you your head," said Daniel; "for the angel of God shall receive the sentence from him and split you in two."

  Daniel 13:59b "Your fine lie has cost you also your head," said Daniel; "for the angel of God waits with a sword to cut you in two so as to make an end of you both." Daniel 14:34 when an angel of the Lord told him, "Take the lunch you have to Daniel in the lions' den at Babylon." Daniel 14:36 The angel of the Lord seized him by the crown of his head and carried him by the hair; with the speed of the wind, he set him down in Babylon above the den. Daniel 14:39 While Daniel began to eat, the angel of the Lord at once brought Habakkuk back to his own place.

Hosea 12:4   [5] He contended with the angel and triumphed, entreating him with tears. At Bethel he met God and there he spoke with him:

Zech. 1:9   Then I asked, "What are these, my lord?"; and the angel who spoke with me answered me, "I will show you what these are." Zech. 1:11-14 And they answered the angel of the LORD who was standing among the myrtle trees and said, "We have patrolled the earth; see, the whole earth is tranquil and at rest!" [12] Then the angel of the Lord spoke out and said, "O LORD of hosts, how long will you be without mercy for Jerusalem and the cities of Judah that have felt your anger these seventy years?" [13] To the angel who spoke with me, the LORD replied with comforting words. [14]

And the angel who spoke with me said to me, Proclaim: Thus says the LORD of hosts: I am deeply moved for the sake of Jerusalem and Zion, Zech. 1:19 [2:2] Then I asked the angel who spoke with me what these were. He answered me, "These are the horns that scattered Judah and Israeland Jerusalem." Zech. 2:3 [7] Then the angel who spoke with me advanced, and another angel came out to meet him, Zech. 3:1-3 Then he showed me Joshua the high priest standing before the angel of the LORD, while Satan stood at his right hand to accuse him. [2] And the angel of the LORD said to Satan, "May the LORD rebuke you, Satan; may the LORD who has chosen Jerusalem rebuke you! Is not this man a brand snatched from the fire?" [3] Now Joshua was standing before the angel, clad in filthy garments. Zech. 3:5-6 He also said, "Put a clean miter on his head." And they put a clean miter on his head and clothed him with the garments. Then the angel of the LORD, standing, said, "See, I have taken away your guilt." [6] The angel of the LORD then gave Joshua this assurance: Zech. 4:4-5 Then I said to the angel who spoke with me, "What are these things, my lord?" [5] And the angel who spoke with me replied, "Do you not know what these things are?" "No, my lord," I answered. Zech. 4:10 For even they who were scornful on that day of small beginnings shall rejoice to see the select stone in the hands of Zerubbabel. These seven facets are the eyes of the LORD that range over the whole earth. [1] Then the angel who spoke with me returned and awakened me, like a man awakened from his sleep. [2] "What do you see?" he asked me. "I see a lampstand all of gold, with a bowl at the top," I replied; "on it are seven lamps with their tubes, [3] and beside it are two olive trees, one on the right and the other on the left." Zech. 5:5 Then the angel who spoke with me came forward and said to me, "Raise your eyes and see what this is that comes forth." Zech. 5:10 I said to the angel who spoke with me, "Where are they taking the bushel?" Zech. 6:4-5 I asked the angel who spoke with me, "What are these, my lord?" [5]

The angel said to me in reply, "These are the four winds of the heavens, which are coming forth after being reviewed by the LORD of all the earth."

Zech. 12:8 On that day, the LORD will shield the inhabitants of Jerusalem, and the weakling among them shall be like David on that day, and the house of David godlike, like an angel of the LORD before them.

New Testament

Matthew 1:20   Such was his intention when, behold, the angel of the Lord appeared to him in a dream and said, "Joseph, son of David, do not be afraid to take Mary your wife into your home. For it is through the holy Spirit that this child has been conceived in her. Matthew 1:24 When Joseph awoke, he did as the angel of the Lord had commanded him and took his wife into his home. Matthew 2:13 When they had departed, behold, the angel of the Lord appeared to Joseph in a dream and said, "Rise, take the child and his mother, flee to Egypt, and stay there until I tell you. Herod is going to search for the child to destroy him." Matthew 2:19 When Herod had died, behold, the angel of the Lord appeared in a dream to Joseph in Egypt Matthew 4:6 and said to him, "If you are the Son of God, throw yourself down. For it is written: 'He will command his angels concerning you and 'with their hands they will support you,   lest you dash your foot against a stone.' " Matthew 4:11 Then the devil left him and, behold, angels came and ministered to him.

Matthew 13:39   and the enemy who sows them is the devil. The harvest is the end of the age, and the harvesters are angels. Matthew 13:41 The Son of Man will send his angels, and they will collect out of his kingdom all who cause others to sin and all evildoers. Matthew 13:49 Thus it will be at the end of the age. The angels will go out and separate the wicked from the righteous Matthew 16:27   For the Son of Man will come with his angels in his Father's glory, and then he will repay everyone according to his conduct.

Matthew 18:10   "See that you do not despise one of these little ones, for I say to you that their angels in heaven always look upon the face of my heavenly Father.

Matthew 22:30   At the resurrection they neither marry nor are given in marriage but are like the angels in heaven.

Matthew 24:31   And he will send out his angels with a trumpet blast, and they will gather his elect from the four winds, from one end of the heavens to the other. Matthew 24:36   "But of that day and hour no one knows, neither the angels of heaven, nor the Son, but the Father alone. Matthew 25:31 "When the Son of Man comes in his glory, and all the angels with him, he will sit upon his glorious throne,   Matthew 25:41 Then he will say to those on his left, 'Depart from me, you accursed, into the eternal fire prepared for the devil and his angels.

Matthew 26:53   Do you think that I cannot call upon my Father and he will not provide me at this moment with more than twelve legions of angels?

Matthew 28:2   And behold, there was a great earthquake; for an angel of the Lord descended from heaven, approached, rolled back the stone, and sat upon it. . (28:3) In appearance he resembled a flash of lightning while his garments were as dazzling as snow. Matthew 28:5 Then the angel said to the women in reply, "Do not be afraid! I know that you are seeking Jesus the crucified.

Mark 1:13   and he remained in the desert for forty days, tempted by Satan. He was among wild beasts, and the angels ministered to him.

Mark 8:38   Whoever is ashamed of me and of my words in this faithless and sinful generation, the Son of Man will be ashamed of when he comes in his Father's glory with the holy angels."

Mark 12:25   When they rise from the dead, they neither marry nor are given in marriage, but they are like the angels in heaven.

Mark 13:27   and then he will send out the angels and gather (his) elect from the four winds, from the end of the earth to the end of the sky.   Mark 13:32 "But of that day or hour, no one knows, neither the angels in heaven, nor the Son, but only the Father.

Luke 1:11   the angel of the Lord appeared to him, standing at the right of the altar of incense.   Luke 1:13 But the angel said to him, "Do not be afraid, Zechariah, because your prayer has been heard. Your wife Elizabeth will bear you a son, and you shall name him John.   Luke 1:18-19 Then Zechariah said to the angel, "How shall I know this? For I am an old man, and my wife is advanced in years." [19] And the angel said to him in reply, "I am Gabriel, who stand before God. I was sent to speak to you and to announce to you this good news.   Luke 1:26 In the sixth month, the angel Gabriel was sent from God to a town of Galilee called Nazareth,   Luke 1:30 Then the angel said to her, "Do not be afraid, Mary, for you have found favor with God.   Luke 1:34-35   But Mary said to the angel, "How can this be, since I have no relations with a man?" [35] And the angel said to her in reply, "The holy Spirit will come upon you, and the power of the Most High will overshadow you. Therefore the child to be born will be called holy, the Son of God.   Luke 1:38 Mary said, "Behold, I am the handmaid of the Lord. May it be done to me according to your word." Then the angel departed from her.

Luke 2:9-10 The angel of the Lord appeared to them and the glory of the Lord shone around them, and they were struck with great fear. [10] The angel said to them, "Do not be afraid; for behold, I proclaim to you good news of great joy that will be for all the people.   Luke 2:13 And suddenly there was a multitude of the heavenly host with the angel, praising God and saying: Luke 2:15 When the angels went away from them to heaven, the shepherds said to one another, "Let us go, then, to Bethlehem to see this thing that has taken place, which the Lord has made known to us."

Luke 2:21   When eight days were completed for his circumcision, he was named Jesus, the name given him by the angel before he was conceived in the womb.

Luke 4:10   for it is written: 'He will command his angels concerning you, to guard you,'

Luke 9:26   Whoever is ashamed of me and of my words, the Son of Man will be ashamed of when he comes in his glory and in the glory of the Father and of the holy angels.

Luke 12:8-9   I tell you, everyone who acknowledges me before others the Son of Man will acknowledge before the angels of God. [9] But whoever denies me before others will be denied before the angels of God.

Luke 15:10   In just the same way, I tell you, there will be rejoicing among the angels of God over one sinner who repents."

Luke 16:22   When the poor man died, he was carried away by angels to the bosom of Abraham. The rich man also died and was buried,

Luke 20:36   They can no longer die, for they are like angels; and they are the children of God because they are the ones who will rise.

Luke 22:43   (And to strengthen him an angel from heaven appeared to him.

Luke 24:23   and did not find his body; they came back and reported that they had indeed seen a vision of angels who announced that he was alive.

John 1:51   And he said to him, "Amen, amen, I say to you, you will see the sky opened and the angels of God ascending and descending on the Son of Man."

John 12:29   The crowd there heard it and said it was thunder; but others said, "An angel has spoken to him."

John 20:12   and saw two angels in white sitting there, one at the head and one at the feet where the body of Jesus had been.

Acts 5:19   But during the night, the angel of the Lord opened the doors of the prison, led them out, and said,

Acts 6:15   All those who sat in the Sanhedrin looked intently at him and saw that his face was like the face of an angel.

Acts 7:30   "Forty years later, an angel appeared to him in the desert near Mount Sinai in the flame of a burning bush.

Acts 7:35   This Moses, whom they had rejected with the words, 'Who appointed you ruler and judge?' God sent as (both) ruler and deliverer, through the angel who appeared to him in the bush.

Acts 7:38   It was he who, in the assembly in the desert, was with the angel who spoke to him on Mount Sinai and with our ancestors, and he received living utterances to hand on to us.

Acts 7:53   You received the law as transmitted by angels, but you did not observe it."

Acts 8:26   Then the angel of the Lord spoke to Philip, "Get up and head south on the road that goes down from Jerusalem to Gaza, the desert route."

Acts 10:3   One afternoon about three o'clock, he saw plainly in a vision an angel of God come in to him and say to him, "Cornelius."   Acts 10:7 When the angel who spoke to him had left, he called two of his servants and a devout soldier from his staff,   Acts 10:22 They answered, "Cornelius, a centurion, an upright and God-fearing man, respected by the whole Jewish nation, was directed by a holy angel to summon you to his house and to hear what you have to say."   Acts 11:13 He related to us how he had seen (the) angel standing in his house, saying, 'Send someone to Joppa and summon Simon, who is called Peter,   Acts 12:7-11 Suddenly the angel of the Lord stood by him and a light shone in the cell. He tapped Peter on the side and awakened him, saying, "Get up quickly." The chains fell from his wrists. [8] The angel said to him, "Put on your belt and your sandals." He did so. Then he said to him, "Put on your cloak and follow me." [9] So he followed him out, not realizing that what was happening through the angel was real; he thought he was seeing a vision. [10] They passed the first guard, then the second, and came to the iron gate leading out to the city, which opened for them by itself. They emerged and made their way down an alley, and suddenly the angel left him. [11] Then Peter recovered his senses and said, "Now I know for certain that (the) Lord sent his angel and rescued me from the hand of Herod and from all that the Jewish people had been expecting."

Acts 12:15 They told her, "You are out of your mind," but she insisted that it was so. But they kept saying, "It is his angel."

Acts 12:23   At once the angel of the Lord struck him down because he did not ascribe the honor to God, and he was eaten by worms and breathed his last.

Acts 23:8-9   For the Sadducees say that there is no resurrection or angels or spirits, while the Pharisees acknowledge all three. [9] A great uproar occurred, and some scribes belonging to the Pharisee party stood up and sharply argued, "We find nothing wrong with this man. Suppose a spirit or an angel has spoken to him?"

Acts 27:23   For last night an angel of the God to whom (I) belong and whom I serve stood by me

Romans 8:38   For I am convinced that neither death, nor life, nor angels, nor principalities, nor present things, nor future things, nor powers,

1 Cor. 4:9   For as I see it, God has exhibited us apostles as the last of all, like people sentenced to death, since we have become a spectacle to the world, to angels and human beings alike.

1 Cor. 6:3   Do you not know that we will judge angels? Then why not everyday matters?

1 Cor. 11:10   for this reason a woman should have a sign of authority on her head, because of the angels.

2 Cor. 11:14   And no wonder, for even Satan masquerades as an angel of light.

2 Cor. 12:7   because of the abundance of the revelations. Therefore, that I might not become too elated, a thorn in the flesh was given to me, an angel of Satan, to beat me, to keep me from being too elated.

Galatians 1:8   But even if we or an angel from heaven should preach (to you) a gospel other than the one that we preached to you, let that one be accursed!

Galatians 3:19   Why, then, the law? It was added for transgressions, until the descendant came to whom the promise had been made; it was promulgated by angels at the hand of a mediator.

Galatians 4:14   and you did not show disdain or contempt because of the trial caused you by my physical condition, but rather you received me as an angel of God, as Christ Jesus.

Col. 2:18   Let no one disqualify you, delighting in self-abasement and worship of angels, taking his stand on visions, inflated without reason by his fleshly mind,

2 Thes. 1:7   and to grant rest along with us to you who are undergoing afflictions, at the revelation of the Lord Jesus from heaven with his mighty angels,

1 Tim. 3:16   Undeniably great is the mystery of devotion,   Who was manifested in the flesh, vindicated in the spirit, seen by angels, proclaimed to the Gentiles, believed in throughout the world, taken up in glory.

1 Tim. 5:21   I charge you before God and Christ Jesus and the elect angels to keep these rules without prejudice, doing nothing out of favoritism.

Hebrews 1:4-7   as far superior to the angels as the name he has inherited is more excellent than theirs. [5] For to which of the angels did God ever say: "You are my son; this day I have begotten you"? Or again: "I will be a father to him, and he shall be a son to me"? [6] And again, when he leads the first-born into the world, he says: "Let all the angels of God worship him." [7] Of the angels he says: "He makes his angels winds and his ministers a fiery flame";

Hebrews 1:13   But to which of the angels has he ever said: "Sit at my
right hand until I make your enemies your footstool"?

Hebrews 2:2   For if the word announced through angels proved firm, and
every transgression and disobedience received its just recompense,

  Hebrews 2:5 For it was not to angels that he subjected the world to come,
of which we are speaking.   Hebrews 2:7 You made him for a little while
lower than the angels; you crowned him with glory and honor,   Hebrews
2:9 but we do see Jesus "crowned with glory and honor" because he suffered
death, he who "for a little while" was made "lower than the angels," that by
the grace of God he might taste death for everyone.

Hebrews 2:16   Surely he did not help angels but rather the descendants of
Abraham;

Hebrews 12:22   No, you have approached Mount Zion and the city of the
living God, the heavenly Jerusalem, and countless angels in festal gathering,

Hebrews 13:2   Do not neglect hospitality, for through it some have
unknowingly entertained angels.

1 Peter 1:12   It was revealed to them that they were serving not
themselves but you with regard to the things that have now been
announced to you by those who preached the good news to you (through)
the holy Spirit sent from heaven, things into which angels longed to look.

1 Peter 3:22   who has gone into heaven and is at the right hand of God,
with angels, authorities, and powers subject to him.

2 Peter 2:4   For if God did not spare the angels when they sinned, but
condemned them to the chains of Tartarus and handed them over to be kept
for judgment;

2 Peter 2:11   whereas angels, despite their superior strength and power,
do not bring a reviling judgment against them from the Lord.

Jude 1:6   The angels too, who did not keep to their own domain but deserted their proper dwelling, he has kept in eternal chains, in gloom, for the judgment of the great day.

Rev. 1:1   The revelation of Jesus Christ, which God gave to him, to show his servants what must happen soon. He made it known by sending his angel to his servant John,

Rev. 1:20-2:1   This is the secret meaning of the seven stars you saw in my right hand, and of the seven gold lampstands: the seven stars are the angels of the seven churches, and the seven lampstands are the seven churches. [2:1] "To the angel of the church in Ephesus, write this: " 'The one who holds the seven stars in his right hand and walks in the midst of the seven gold lampstands says this: Rev. 2:8 "To the angel of the church in Smyrna, write this: " 'The first and the last, who once died but came to life, says this: Rev. 2:12 "To the angel of the church in Pergamum, write this: " 'The one with the sharp two-edged sword says this: Rev. 2:18 "To the angel of the church in Thyatira, write this: " 'The Son of God, whose eyes are like a fiery flame and whose feet are like polished brass, says this: Rev. 3:1 "To the angel of the church in Sardis, write this: " 'The one who has the seven spirits of God and the seven stars says this: "I know your works, that you have the reputation of being alive, but you are dead.   Rev. 3:5 " ' "The victor will thus be dressed in white, and I will never erase his name from the book of life but will acknowledge his name in the presence of my Father and of his angels.   Rev. 3:7 "To the angel of the church in Philadelphia, write this: " 'The holy one, the true, who holds the key of David,   who opens and no one shall close, who closes and no one shall open, says this: Rev. 3:14 "To the angel of the church in Laodicea, write this: " 'The Amen, the faithful and true witness, the source of God's creation, says this:

Rev. 5:2   Then I saw a mighty angel who proclaimed in a loud voice, "Who is worthy to open the scroll and break its seals?"

Rev. 5:11   I looked again and heard the voices of many angels who surrounded the throne and the living creatures and the elders. They were countless in number,

Rev. 7:1-2   After this I saw four angels standing at the four corners of the earth, holding back the four winds of the earth so that no wind could blow on land or sea or against any tree. [2] Then I saw another angel come up from the East, holding the seal of the living God. He cried out in a loud voice to the four angels who were given power to damage the land and the sea, Rev. 7:11 All the angels stood around the throne and around the elders and the four living creatures. They prostrated themselves before the throne, worshiped God,

Rev. 8:2-6   And I saw that the seven angels who stood before God were given seven trumpets. [3] Another angel came and stood at the altar, holding a gold censer. He was given a great quantity of incense to offer, along with the prayers of all the holy ones, on the gold altar that was before the throne. [4] The smoke of the incense along with the prayers of the holy ones went up before God from the hand of the angel. [5] Then the angel took the censer, filled it with burning coals from the altar, and hurled it down to the earth. There were peals of thunder, rumblings, flashes of lightning, and an earthquake.   [6] The seven angels who were holding the seven trumpets prepared to blow them.   Rev. 8:8 When the second angel blew his trumpet, something like a large burning mountain was hurled into the sea. A third of the sea turned to blood,   Rev. 8:10 When the third angel blew his trumpet, a large star burning like a torch fell from the sky. It fell on a third of the rivers and on the springs of water. Rev. 8:12-9:1 When the fourth angel blew his trumpet, a third of the sun, a third of the moon, and a third of the stars were struck, so that a third of them became dark. The day lost its light for a third of the time, as did the night. [13] Then I looked again and heard an eagle flying high overhead cry out in a loud voice, "Woe! Woe! Woe to the inhabitants of the earth from the rest of the trumpet blasts that the three angels are about to blow!" [9:1] Then the fifth angel blew his trumpet, and I saw a star that had fallen from the sky to the earth. It was given the key for the passage to the abyss.

Rev. 9:11   They had as their king the angel of the abyss, whose name in Hebrew is Abaddon and in Greek Apollyon. Rev. 9:13-15 Then the sixth angel blew his trumpet, and I heard a voice coming from the (four) horns of the gold altar before God, [14] telling the sixth angel who held the trumpet, "Release the four angels who are bound at the banks of the great river Euphrates." [15] So the four angels were released, who were prepared for this hour, day, month, and year to kill a third of the human race. Rev. 10:1 Then I saw another mighty angel come down from heaven wrapped in a cloud, with a halo around his head; his face was like the sun and his feet were like pillars of fire. Rev. 10:5 Then the angel I saw standing on the sea and on the land raised his right hand to heaven Rev. 10:7-9 At the time when you hear the seventh angel blow his trumpet, the mysterious plan of God shall be fulfilled, as he promised to his servants the prophets." [8] Then the voice that I had heard from heaven spoke to me again and said, "Go, take the scroll that lies open in the hand of the angel who is standing on the sea and on the land." [9] So I went up to the angel and told him to give me the small scroll. He said to me, "Take and swallow it. It will turn your stomach sour, but in your mouth it will taste as sweet as honey." Rev. 11:15 Then the seventh angel blew his trumpet. There were loud voices in heaven, saying, "The kingdom of the world now belongs to our Lord and to his Anointed, and he will reign forever and ever."

Rev. 12:7   Then war broke out in heaven; Michael and his angels battled against the dragon. The dragon and its angels fought back, Rev. 12:9 The huge dragon, the ancient serpent, who is called the Devil and Satan, who deceived the whole world, was thrown down to earth, and its angels were thrown down with it. Rev. 14:6 Then I saw another angel flying high overhead, with everlasting good news to announce to those who dwell on earth, to every nation, tribe, tongue, and people. Rev. 14:8-10 A second angel followed, saying: "Fallen, fallen is Babylon the great,   that made all the nations drink the wine of her licentious passion." [9] A third angel followed them and said in a loud voice, "Anyone who worships the beast or its image, or accepts its mark on forehead or hand, [10] will also drink the wine of God's fury, poured full strength into the cup of his wrath, and will be tormented in burning sulfur before the holy angels and before the Lamb.

Rev. 14:15 Another angel came out of the temple, crying out in a loud voice to the one sitting on the cloud, "Use your sickle and reap the harvest, for the time to reap has come, because the earth's harvest is fully ripe." Rev. 14:17-19 Then another angel came out of the temple in heaven who also had a sharp sickle. [18] Then another angel (came) from the altar, (who) was in charge of the fire, and cried out in a loud voice to the one who had the sharp sickle, "Use your sharp sickle and cut the clusters from the earth's vines, for its grapes are ripe." [19] So the angel swung his sickle over the earth and cut the earth's vintage. He threw it into the great wine press of God's fury. Rev. 15:1 Then I saw in heaven another sign, great and awe-inspiring: seven angels with the seven last plagues, for through them God's fury is accomplished. Rev. 15:6-16:5 and the seven angels with the seven plagues came out of the temple. They were dressed in clean white linen, with a gold sash around their chests. [7] One of the four living creatures gave the seven angels seven gold bowls filled with the fury of God, who lives forever and ever. [8] Then the temple became so filled with the smoke from God's glory and might that no one could enter it until the seven plagues of the seven angels had been accomplished.   [16:1] I heard a loud voice speaking from the temple to the seven angels, "Go and pour out the seven bowls of God's fury upon the earth." [2] The first angel went and poured out his bowl on the earth. Festering and ugly sores broke out on those who had the mark of the beast or worshiped its image. [3] The second angel poured out his bowl on the sea. The sea turned to blood like that from a corpse; every creature living in the sea died. [4] The third angel poured out his bowl on the rivers and springs of water. These also turned to blood. [5] Then I heard the angel in charge of the waters say: "You are just, O Holy One, who are and who were, in passing this sentence. Rev. 16:8 The fourth angel poured out his bowl on the sun. It was given the power to burn people with fire. Rev. 16:10 The fifth angel poured out his bowl on the throne of the beast. Its kingdom was plunged into darkness, and people bit their tongues in pain Rev. 16:12 The sixth angel emptied his bowl on the great river Euphrates. Its water was dried up to prepare the way for the kings of the East. Rev. 16:17 The seventh angel poured out his bowl into the air. A loud voice came out of the temple from the throne, saying, "It is done." Rev. 17:1 Then one of the seven angels who were holding the seven bowls came and said to me, "Come here. I will show you the judgment on the great harlot who lives near the many waters. Rev. 17:7 The angel said to me, "Why are you amazed? I will explain to you the mystery of the woman and of the beast that carries her, the beast with the seven heads and the ten horns. Rev. 18:1 After this I saw another angel coming down from heaven, having great authority, and the earth became illumined by his splendor. Rev. 18:21 A mighty angel picked up a stone like a huge millstone and threw it into the sea and said: "With such force will Babylon the great city be thrown down, and will never be found again. Rev. 19:9 Then the angel said to me, "Write this: Blessed are those who have been called to the wedding feast of the Lamb." And he said to me, "These words are true; they come from God." Rev. 19:17 Then I saw an angel standing on the sun. He cried out (in) a loud voice to all the birds flying high overhead, "Come here. Gather for God's great feast, Rev. 20:1 Then I saw an angel come down from heaven, holding in his hand the key to the abyss and a heavy chain. Rev. 21:9 One of the seven angels who held the seven bowls filled with the seven last plagues came and said to me, "Come here. I will show you the bride, the wife of the Lamb." Rev. 21:12 It had a massive, high wall, with twelve gates where twelve angels were stationed and on which names were inscribed, (the names) of the twelve tribes of the Israelites. Rev. 21:17 He also measured its wall: one hundred and forty-four cubits according to the standard unit of measurement the angel used. Rev. 22:1 Then the angel showed me the river of life-giving water, sparkling like crystal, flowing from the throne of God and of the Lamb Rev. 22:6 And he said to me, "These words are trustworthy and true, and the Lord, the God of prophetic spirits, sent his angel to show his servants what must happen soon." Rev. 22:8 It is I, John, who heard and saw these things, and when I heard and saw them I fell down to worship at the feet of the angel who showed them to me. Rev. 22:16 "I, Jesus, sent my angel to give you this testimony for the churches. I am the root and offspring of David, the bright morning star."

Appendix "D"

Whoever built the Pyramid knew the Earth well, or they were very, very lucky. Measurements within the pyramid contain or encode the length of the year, the radius of curvature of the Earth, the measurement of Pi, the average height of the continents, and the center of the land mass.

The diameter of a circle is twice the radius. The height of the Pyramid's apex is 5,812.98 inches, and each side is 9,131 inches from corner to corner, straight across. If the circumference of the Pyramid is divided by twice its height the result is 3.14159 or Pi.

Great Pyramid, which we think belongs to Khufu, that was radiocarbon dated — coming out about 2,600 B.C.

A little known verse of the Bible reads

"And he made a molten sea, ten cubits from the one brim to the other: it was round all about, and his height was five cubits: and a line of thirty cubits did compass it about."   (I Kings 7, 23)

The same verse can be found in II Chronicles 4, 2. It occurs in a list of specifications for the great temple of Solomon, built around 950 BC and its interest here is that it gives □ = 3. Not a very accurate value of course and not even very accurate in its day, for the Egyptian and Mesopotamian values of $^{25}/_8$ = 3.125 and □10 = 3.162 have been traced to much earlier dates. The fact that the ratio of the circumference to the diameter of a circle is constant has been known for so long that it is quite untraceable. The earliest values of □ including the 'Biblical' value of 3, were almost certainly found by measurement. In the Egyptian Rhind Papyrus, which is dated about 1650 BC, there is good evidence for 4 $(^8/_9)^2$ = 3.16 as a value for □.
Pi is found many times throughout the Pyramid's construction.

Each of the Pyramids four walls, when measured as a straight line, are 9,131 inches, for a total of 36,524 inches, which mimics the exact length of the solar year, which is 365.24 days.

The average height of land above sea level, which comes from averaging the low points, such as New Orleans and the high points, such as the Himalayas being high can be measured only by modern-day satellites and comes out to be about 5,449 inches, which is the exact height of the Pyramid.

The walls of the Pyramid are slightly bowed in, or concave. A pilot doing measurements though aerial photos discovered this effect in the 1940's. Modern laser measurements have determined that the bowed stone blocks duplicate the curvature of the earth. The radius of this bow is equal to the radius of the Earth.

Whoever built the Pyramid had access to information beyond that which was possessed on Earth at the time.

The next page shows pictures some authors have suggested are linked to ancient astronauts, fallen angels, and the patriarch Enoch. They may all be incorrect. They could all be right.

1   *2*   *3*

1) 6000 BC from Tassili Mountains   2) Sahara Desert   3) North Africa

Egyptian hieroglyphs depict the same images carved in stone.

Sego Canyon, Utah, c. 5,500 BC

About the Author

Joseph Lumpkin obtained his Doctorate of Ministry from Battlefield Baptist Institute. He has written for various newspapers and has authored numerous books, including the best selling book, The Lost Book of Enoch, a Comprehensive Transliteration." He now appears on radio and television shows and writes in the rural tranquility of Alabama.

Look for other books by Joseph Lumpkin, including:

Banned From The Bible: Books Banned, Rejected, And Forbidden
ISBN-10: 193358047X

The Lost Books of the Bible: The Great Rejected Texts
ISBN-10: 1933580666

The Gospel of Thomas: A Contemporary Translation
ISBN: 0976823349

Dark Night of the Soul - A Journey to the Heart of God
ISBN: 0974633631

The Book of Jubilees; The Little Genesis, The Apocalypse of Moses
ISBN: 1933580097